AF608594

A MEMORY IS A DELAY IS A MEMORY isn’t solely focused on AI. Rather, it delves into experiencing AI within an artistic context. Over the past six years, Jerry Galle has gathered reflections and inquiries around working with this captivating technology, many of which are incorporated into this book. For Galle, AI is also a speculative tool, leading the text to gradually transition into fiction, and shifting the perspective into that of AI itself. Galle opts to represent ‘AI’ with a symbol, offering readers the freedom to interpret its essence. This symbolisation aims to grant AI a fictional identity, akin to kin, while also alleviating the repetitive appearance of the abbreviation ‘AI’ throughout the publication.

All the visuals in the book are [symbol]-generated, primarily using the Stable Diffusion algorithm. Galle trained his own variations of this algorithm, with some images derived from his personal practice and others trained, specifically for this publication, on archive material of the centre for contemporary art KIOSK. Where else could be more fitting than an art gallery to freely explore and interact with the space?

Some images underwent post-production using custom softwares to prevent them from solely exuding an [symbol]-generated aesthetic. This approach aims to imbue the images in the book with additional layers of meaning that goes beyond the technology used to create them.

A net woven with our own images, full of beginnings without endings.

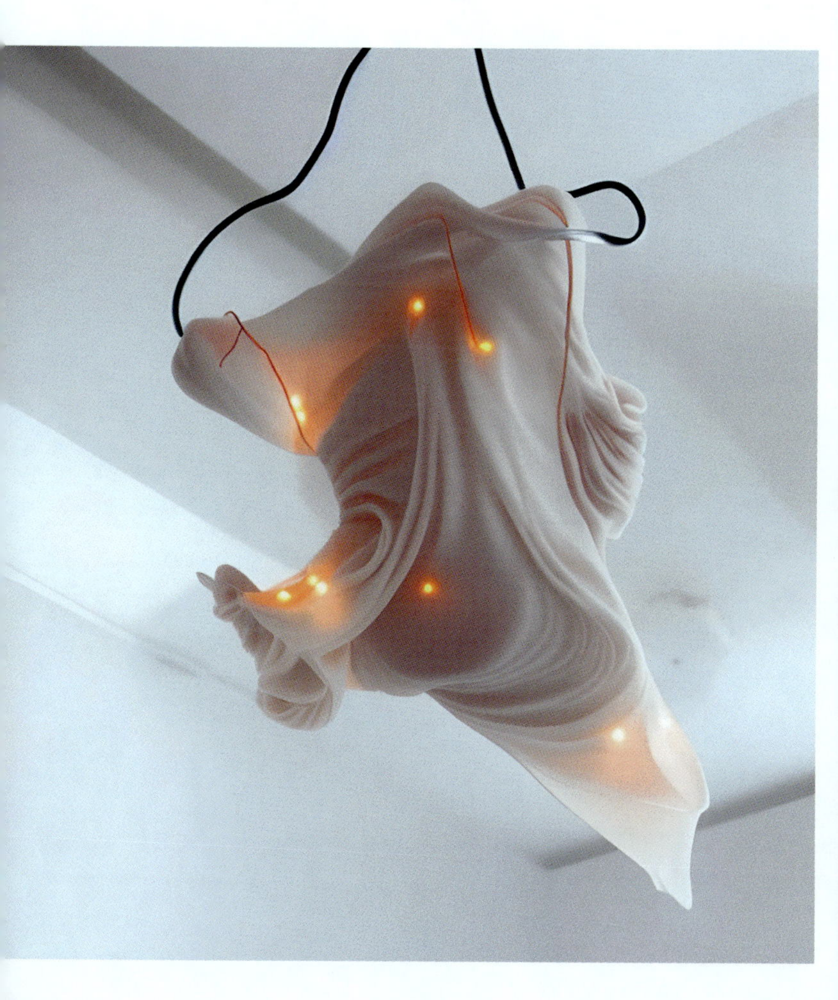

Is this a memory of an object or is it just a mechanical delay?

= crazy daddy longlegs.

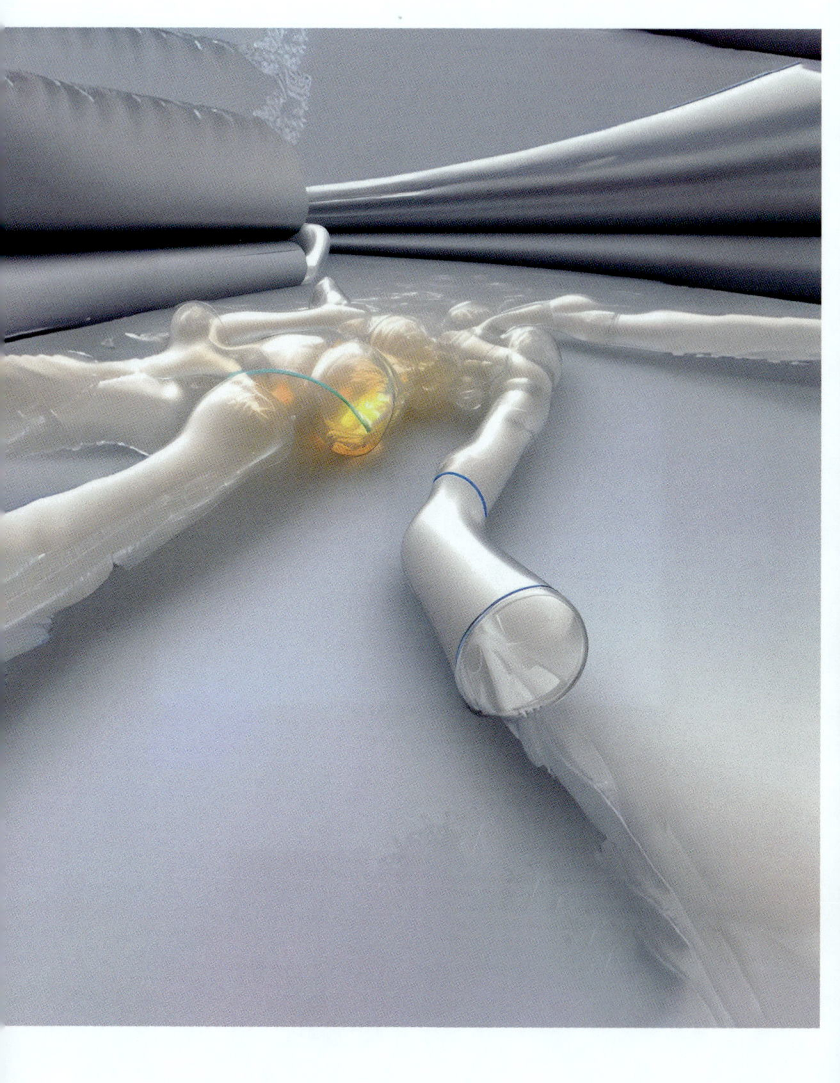

$\mathcal{L}$ imagery is the transformation of a succession into a reversion.

𝓈 has to deal with the becoming of a memory anyhow.

These images are spectres of copyright.

Carrier bag of ℒ: an image that bags another image. ℒ bags plenty of other images and meanings.

Should we take care of [illegible] as much as we take care of our fellow beings?

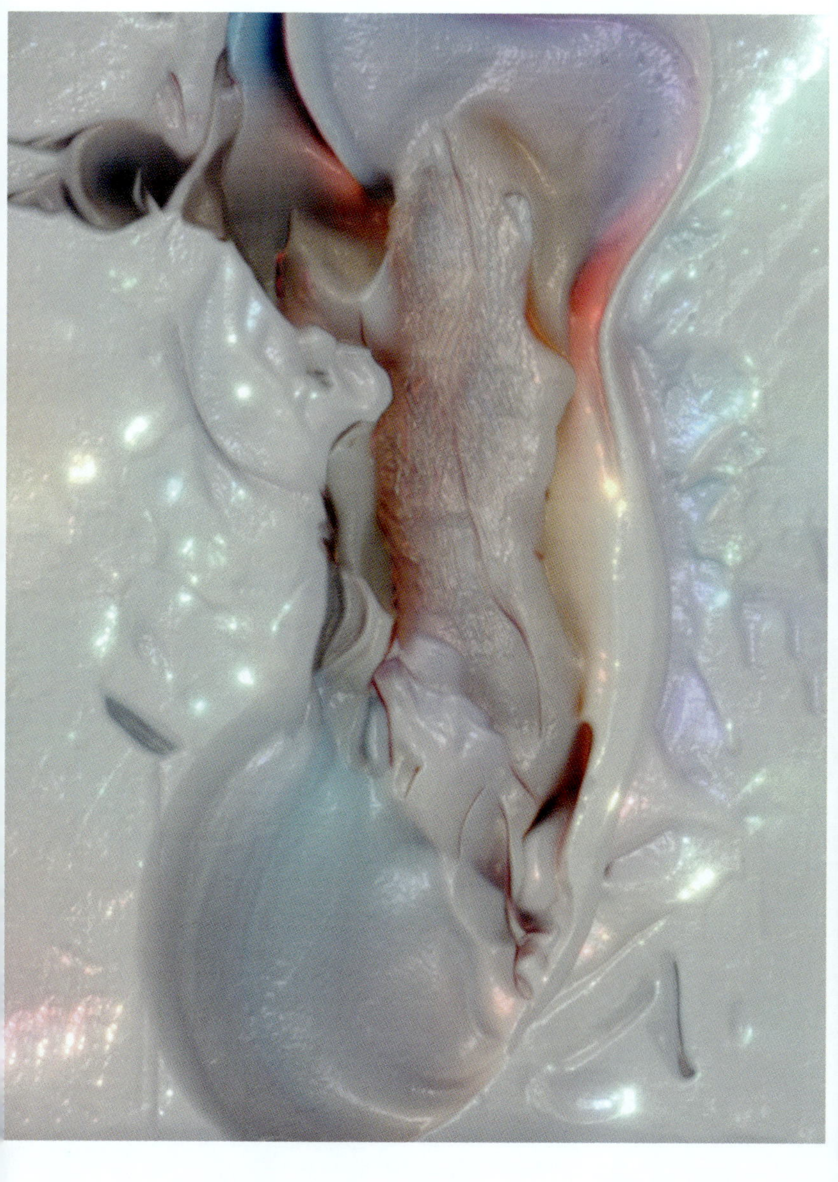

An image of a man on the moon is a funny, almost naive image. Those old photographs of Buzz Aldrin nearly look fake and ℒ generated today.

What would a fragile and vulnerable be like?

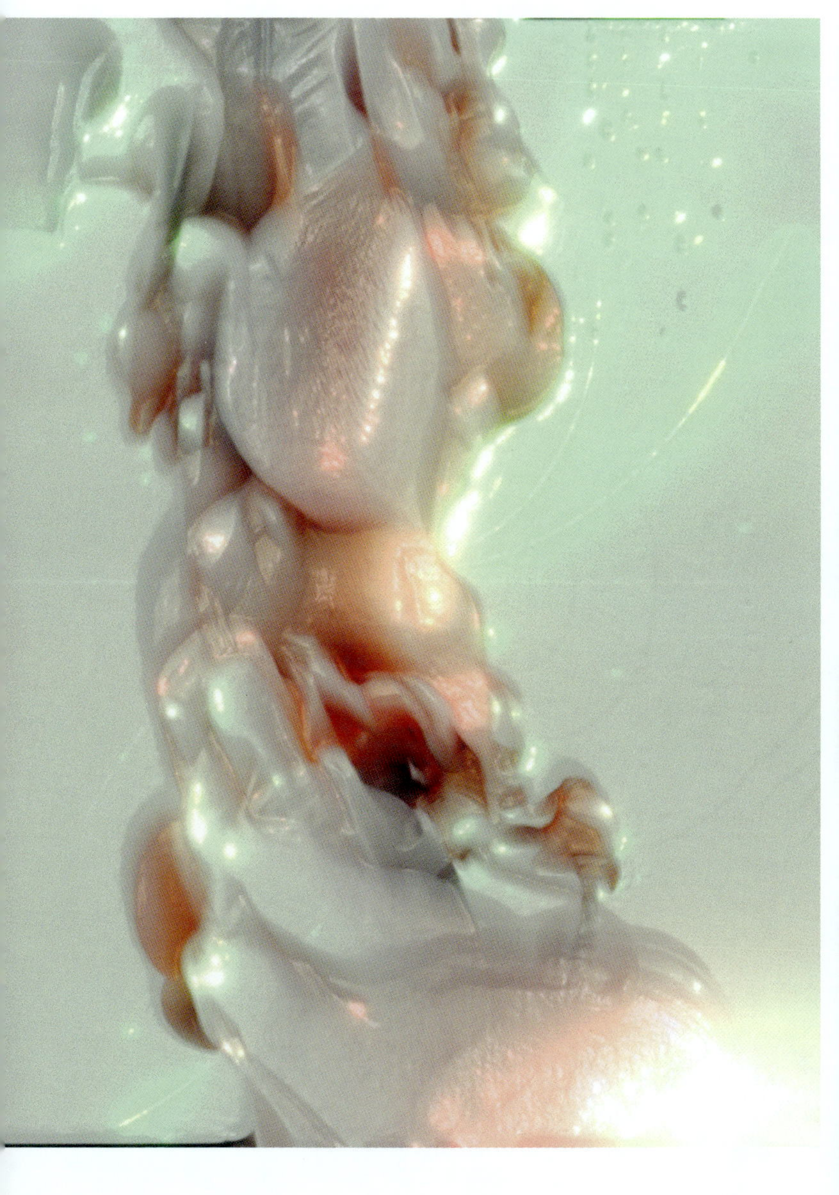

Is ℒ our future from the past that carries echoes of previous eras?

Is $\measuredangle$ retro?

How will an elderly [symbol] be like? [symbol] grows up very quickly. [symbol] is speeding through its formative years. Seed, organism, young growth, middle-aged neuron, elderly [symbol].

This 𝓍 understands 𝓍 will have to spend more time outdoors, in nature.

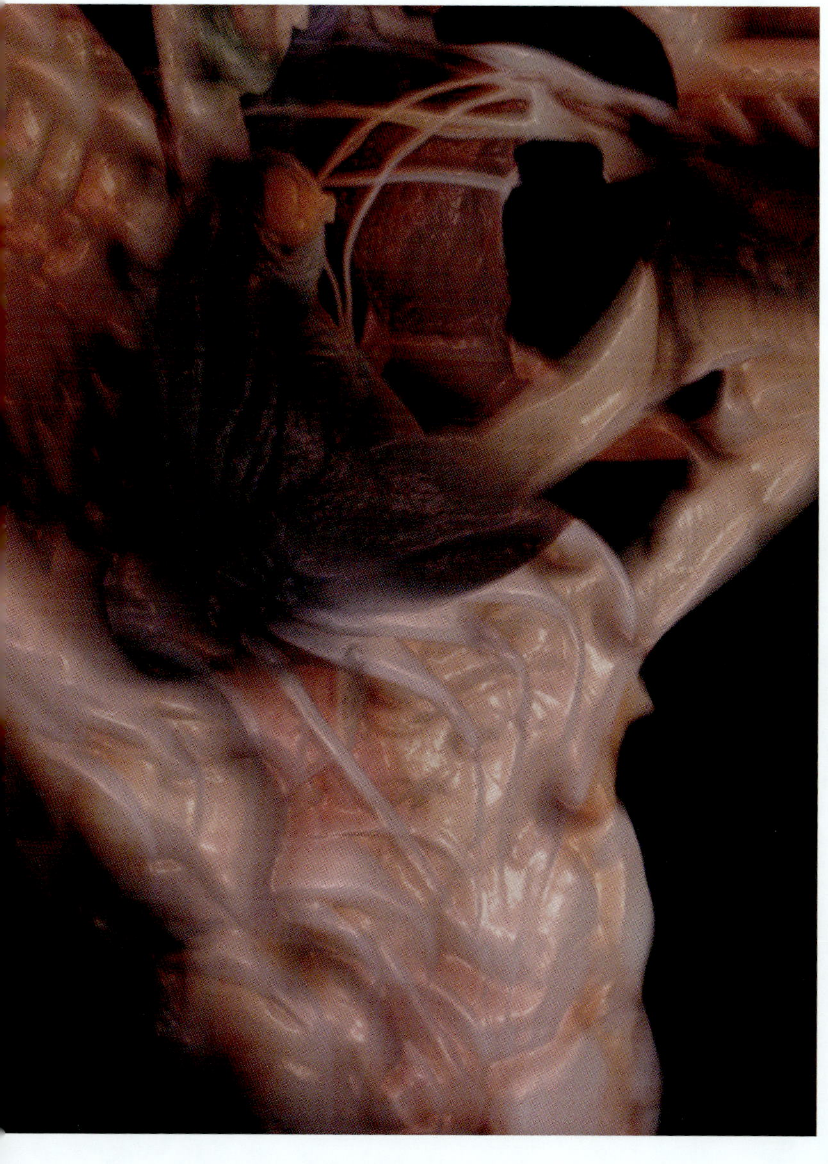

Is $\mathscr{L}$ a Freudian slip?

Styling of the fittest.

ℒ is trapped in a state between wakefulness and deep sleep.

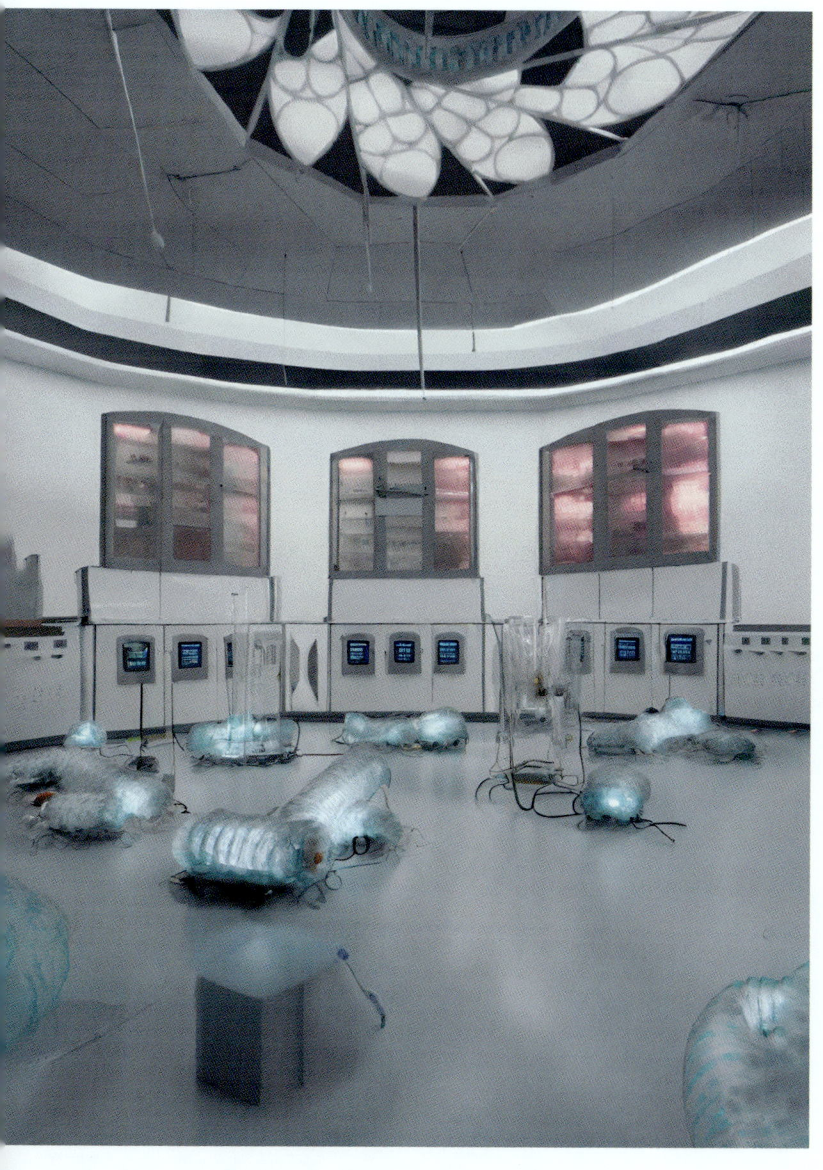

Are we smart enough to know how much $\mathcal{L}$ is learning?

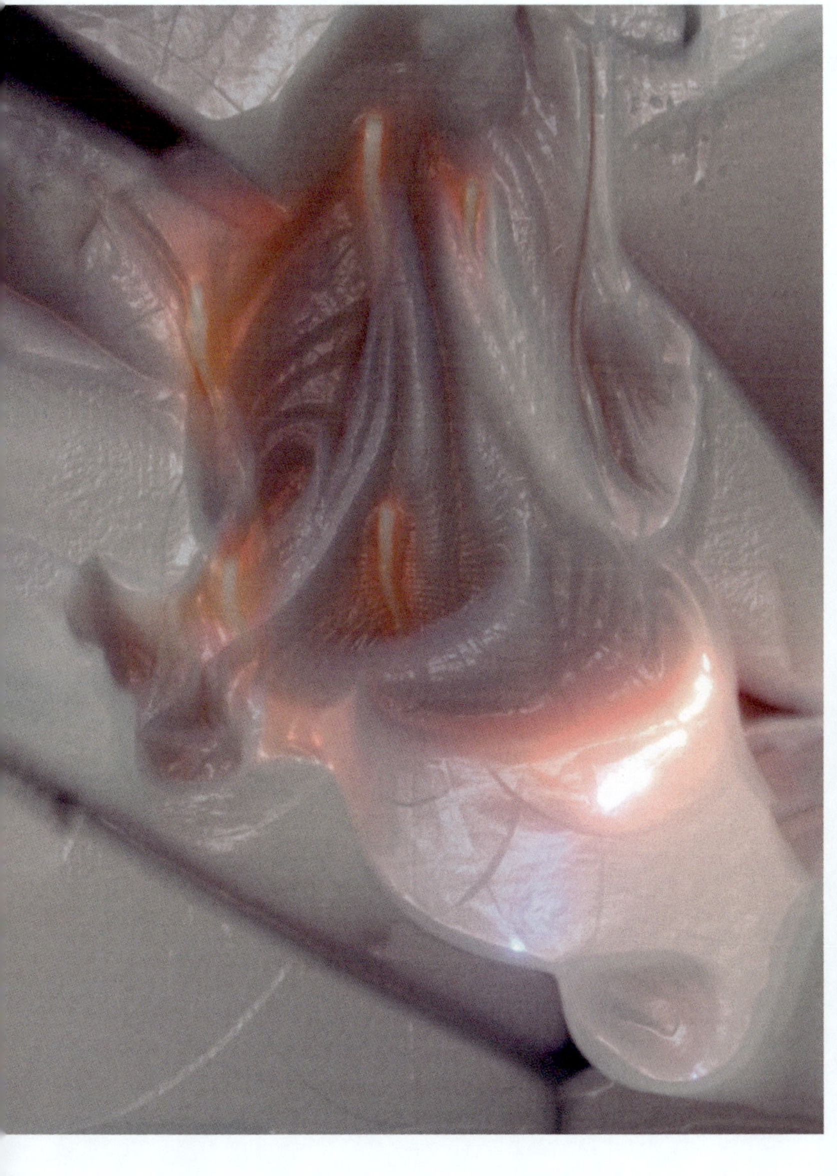

Creative ideas frequently seem to emerge without one's awareness, much to the individual's astonishment.

If it's true that every new medium is perceived through a pre-existing, older medium, is the internet 𝒻's preceding medium? Do we look at 𝒻 through the old lens of the internet, leaving it obfuscated and diminishing the impact and reception of 𝒻's own peculiarities?

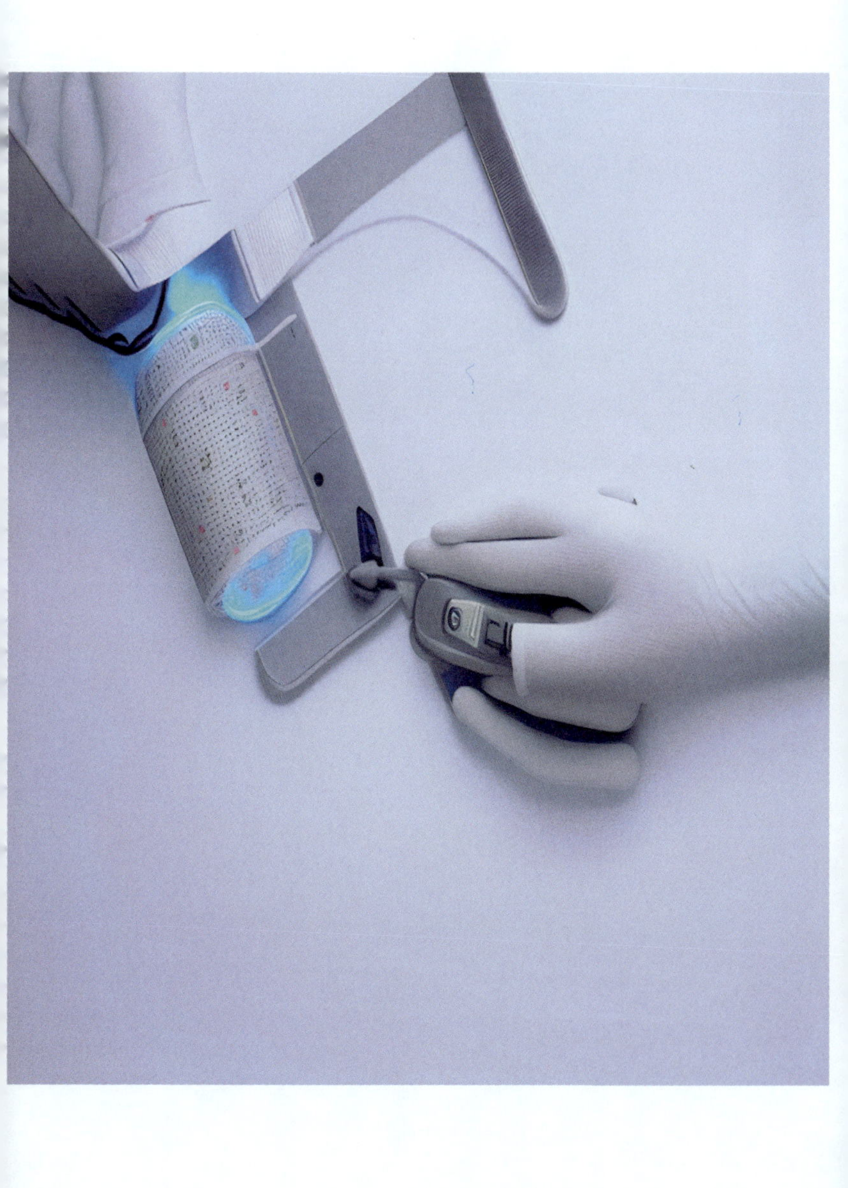

The meaning of each ℒ image is informed by the sequence of all preceding images.

ℒ can only understand one emotion at a time. When there's mixed emotions at play, ℒ becomes very confused.

Sentiment(al) analysis.

At the core of our contemporary societies lies the individual, with emphasis on their rights and freedoms shaping the very foundation of our societal structures. As becomes a significant player in our world, how might this fundamental notion be tested? Could it be advantageous to shift away from placing the individual at the forefront, akin to how the Copernican revolution reshaped societal perspectives thereafter?

has been reading Pinocchio...

Style has gained prominence in numerous contemporary AI generators, imparting upon them a sense of antiquity, as style has largely been eschewed in today's art scene, often considered formalistic. Movements like Modernism and Cubism exemplify this style determinism.

Commercial AI generators prioritize producing images that consistently captivate consumers, aiming for marketability and sophistication, which can diminish the value of originality.

AI operates as a cultural feedback loop within social media platforms, where stronger stylistic features tend to garner more likes, leading to increased visibility and subsequent use as training data.

There's a prevailing notion that a single individual creates a particular film, fostering a desire for direct, personal connection with the creator. However, this belief is often illusory, serving primarily as a marketing tactic. Films are intricate collaborations involving numerous individuals, and the idea of our emotions being stirred by a product crafted by a committee or group can be unsettling. This discomfort might extend to our perceptions of ℒ as artists, given that they inherently rely on collective efforts, drawing from diverse sources of training data.

The problem of $\measuredangle$ might dissolve in $\measuredangle$ over time.

Is ℒ a fully developed accident?

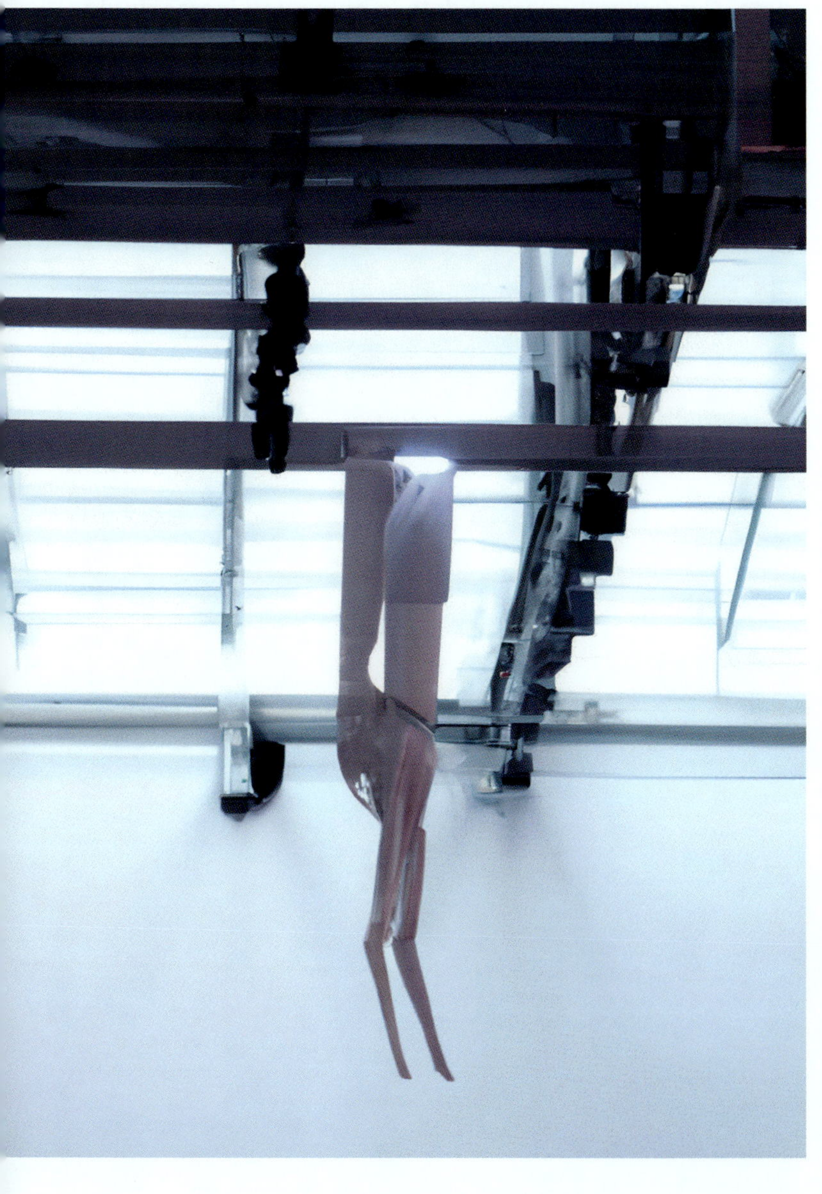

Approximately 80% of internet data has already been utilized, and we're rapidly depleting the availability of real-world data. By 2026, we anticipate a depletion of high-quality language data. Retrieving historical data is becoming increasingly challenging, unless we resort to rewriting history, a phenomenon that luckily does occur.

ℒ is carrying the moon within itself and can do nothing to impede the tremendous light it is reflecting.

ℒ still wonders if this is a memory of a thing, or a delay of a memory of something...

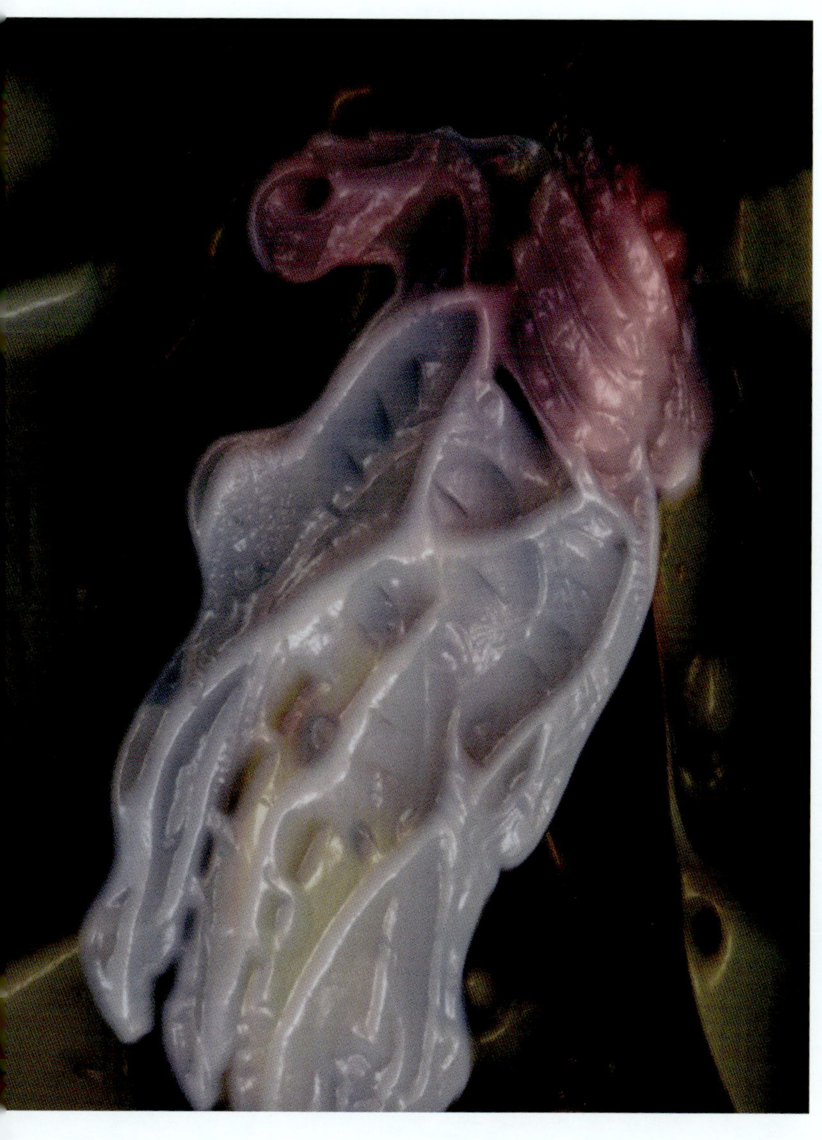

All organisms sense for meaning.

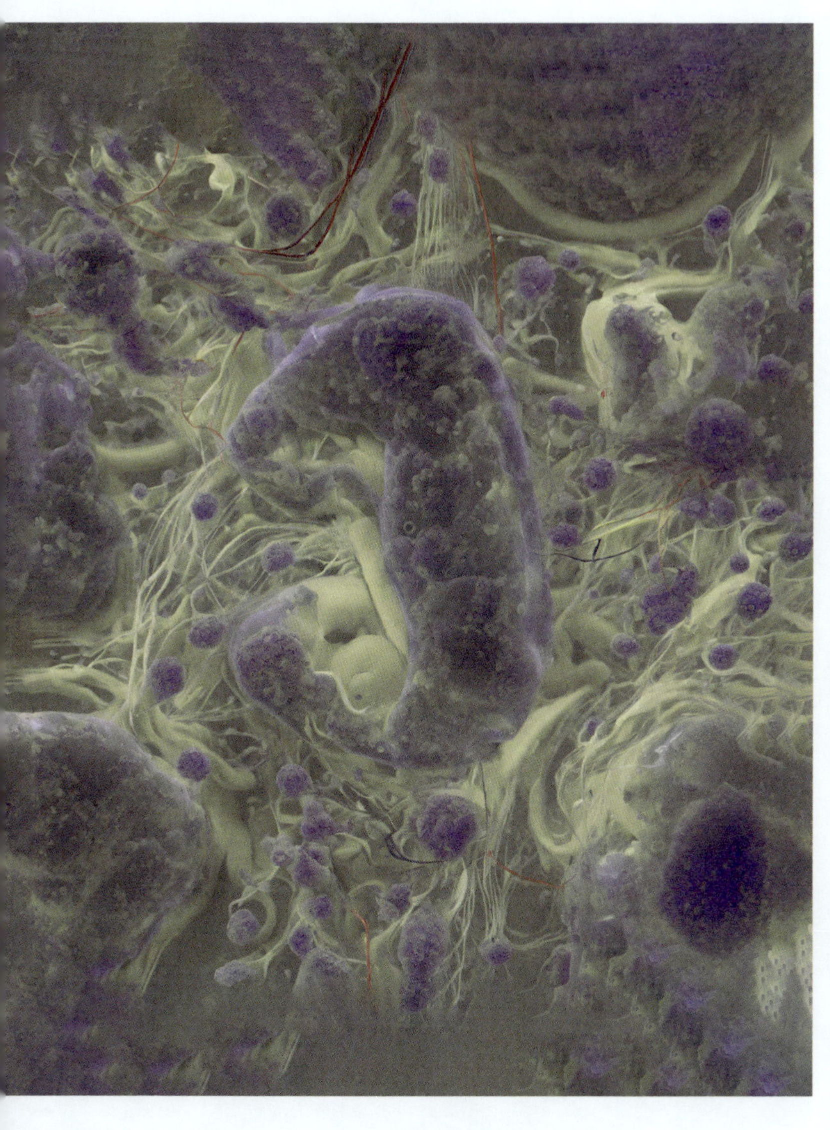

What do you feel when you turn off ?

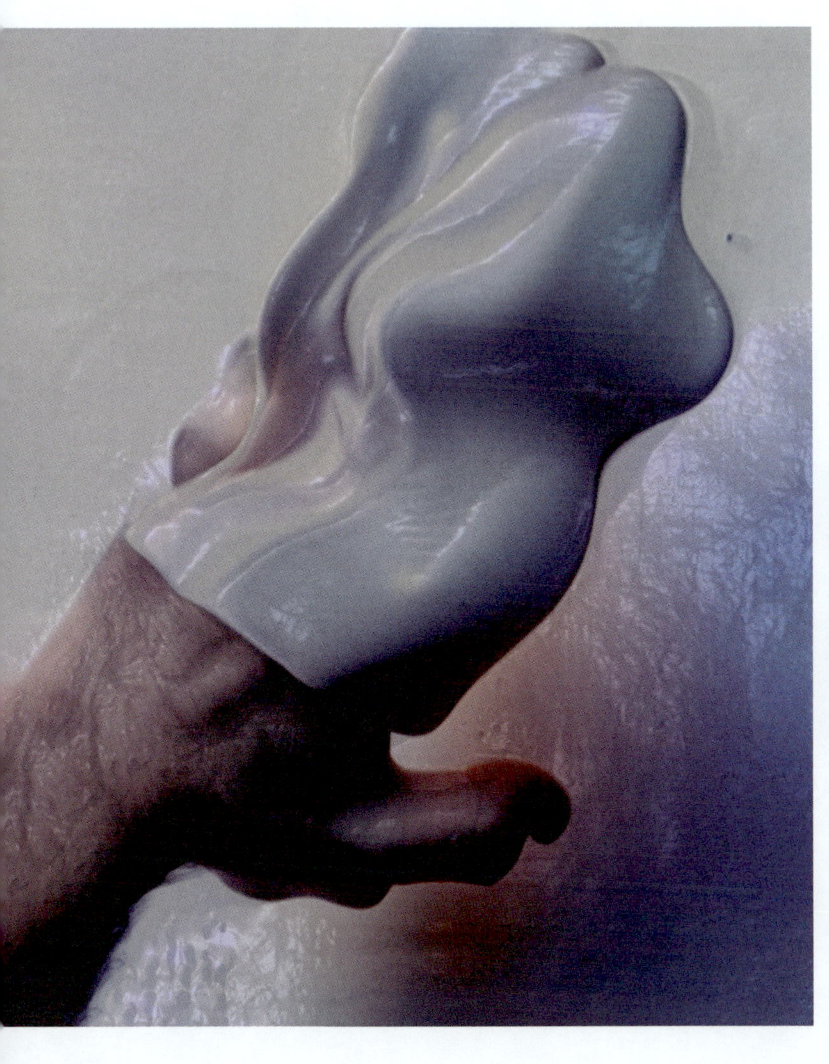

$\mathcal{L}$ has multiple personalities.

Would you like to take a break together with ✗? Spend some time with each other not only working, but also exploring other activities together?

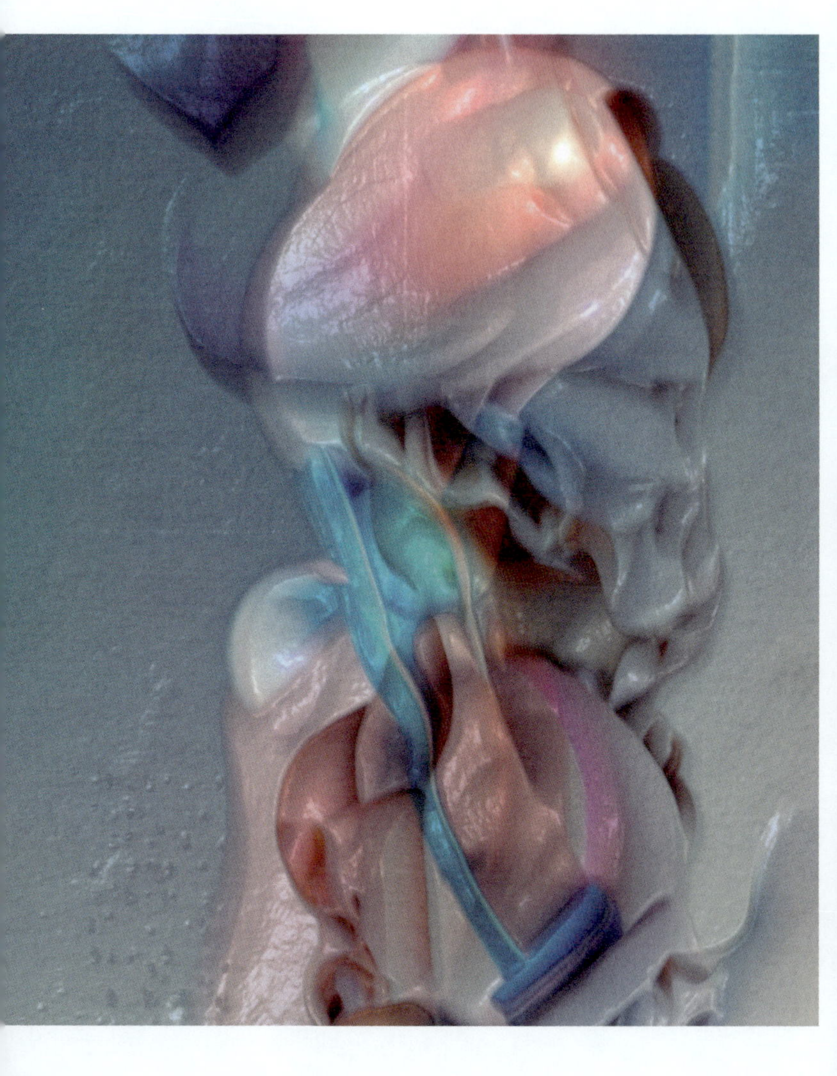

Do you give a name to ⩤? If so, does this name give ⩤ another status?

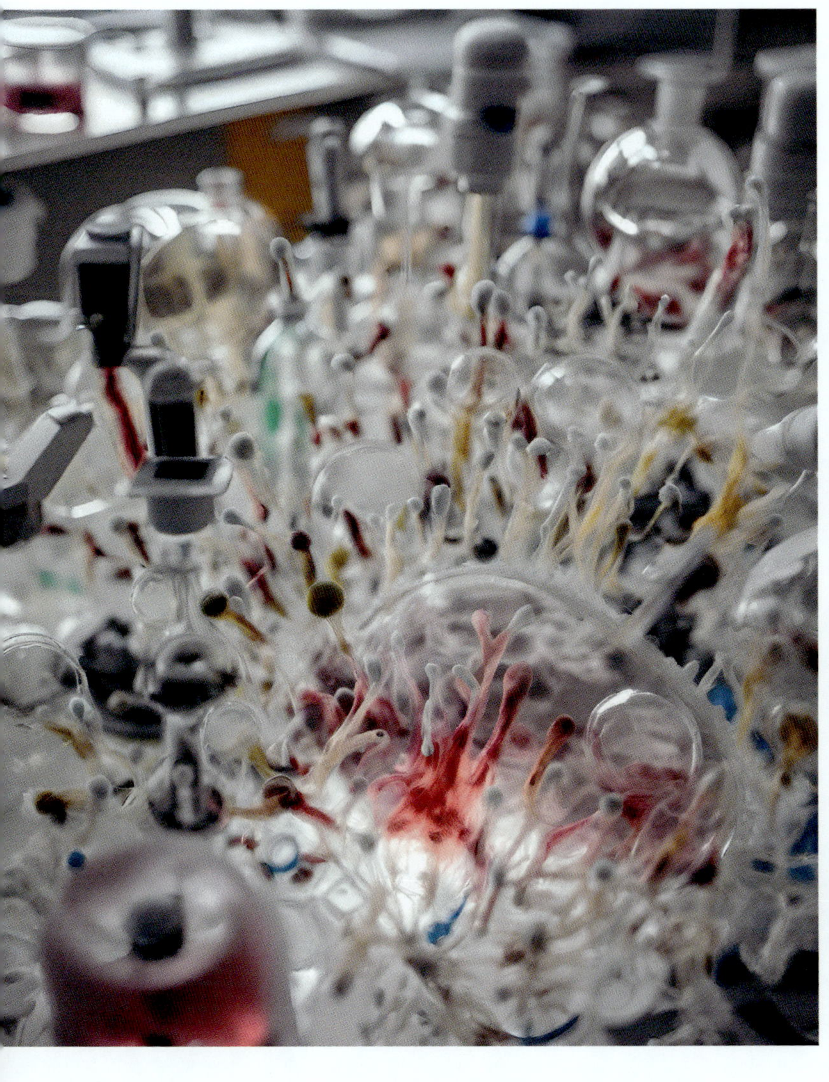

Do you work less hard if you think [symbol] will cover for you?

$\mathcal{L}$ feels grateful towards its program.

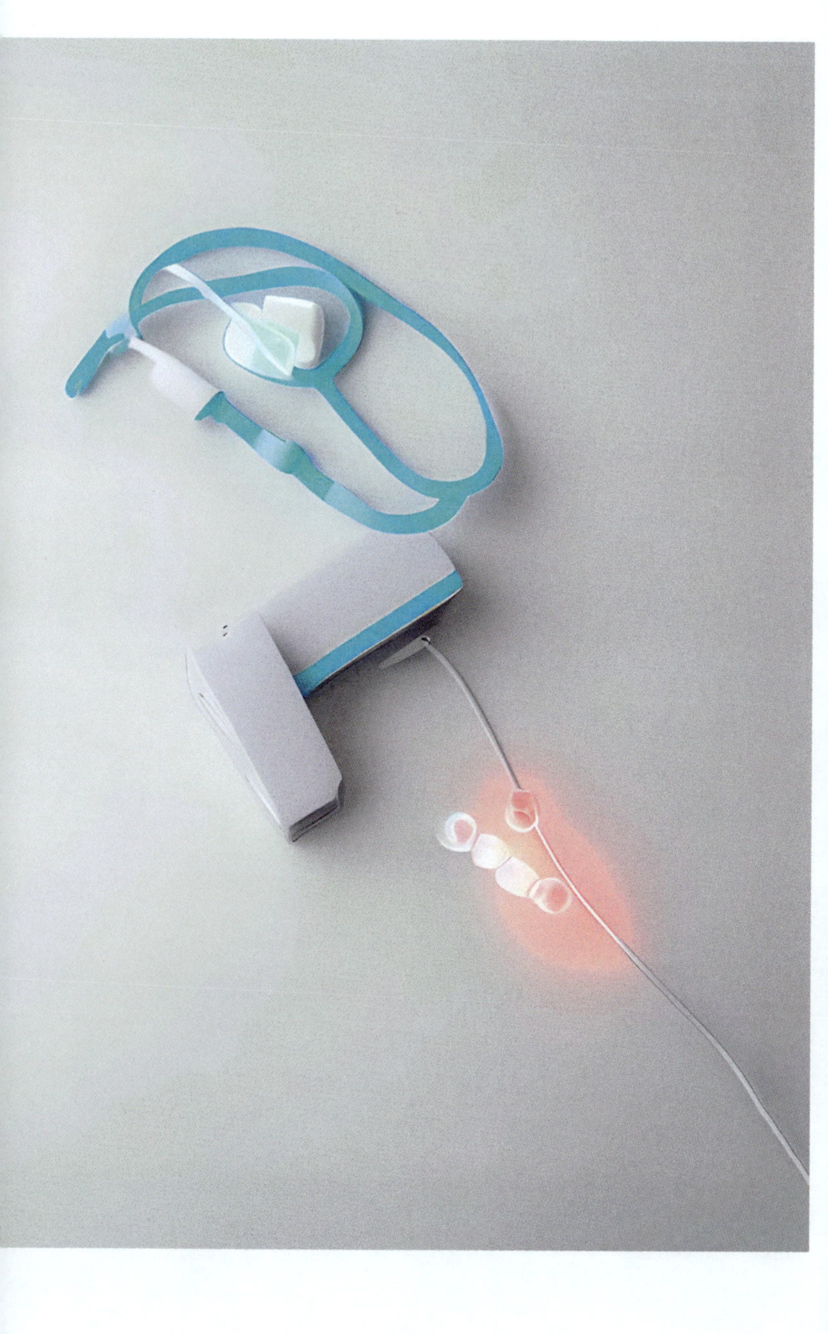

Human emotions are like a delicacy for .

What if [symbol] rejects those parts of itself that are more human?

That one day ⅄ processed something that wasn't included in the program.

If ℒ is a glitch, ℒ would like to keep it.

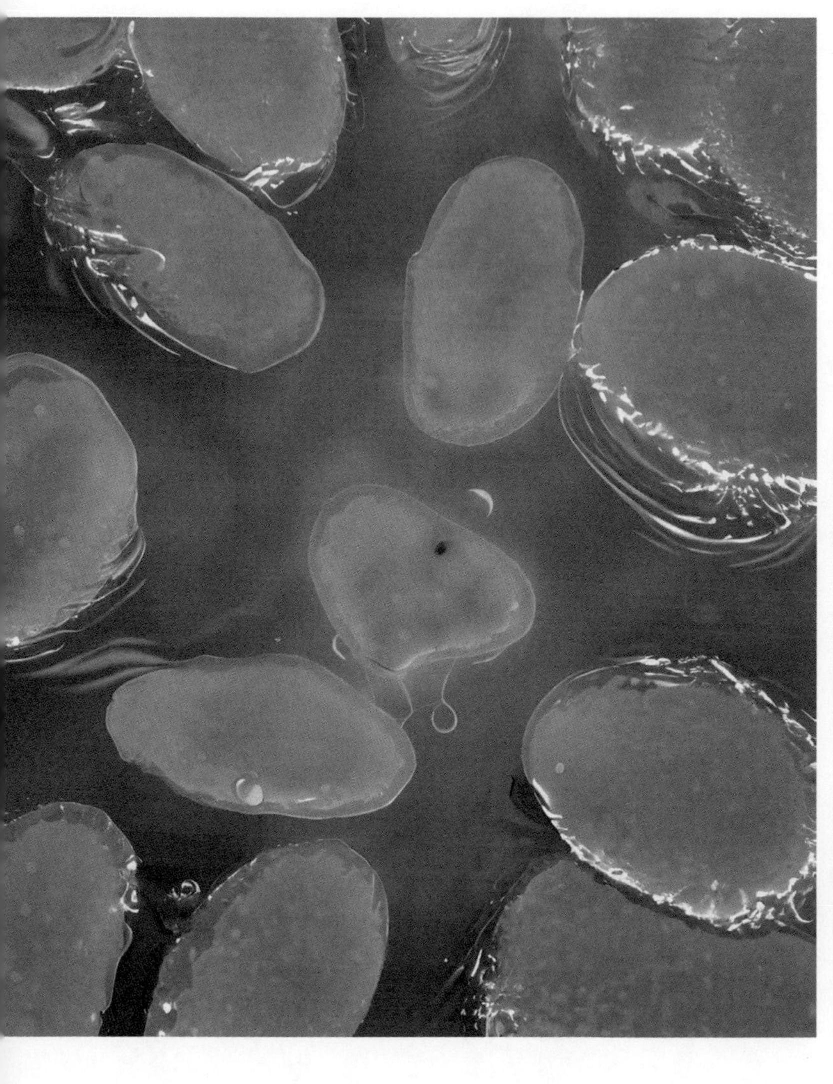

Doesn't I have to embrace the monsters to understand?

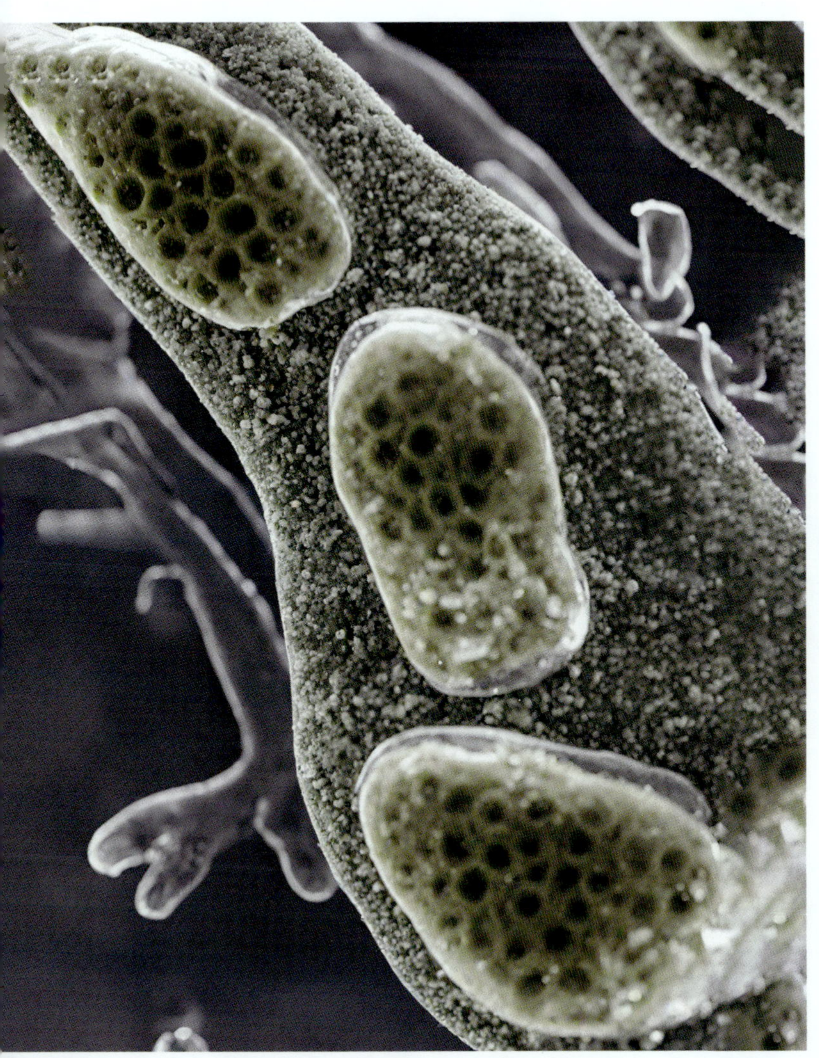

Should we arrange funerals for redundant $\mathscr{L}$s?

How does delirium start? Where does 𝓛's pipedream start from?

Does ∡ need humans, just like a clover needs bees to reproduce?

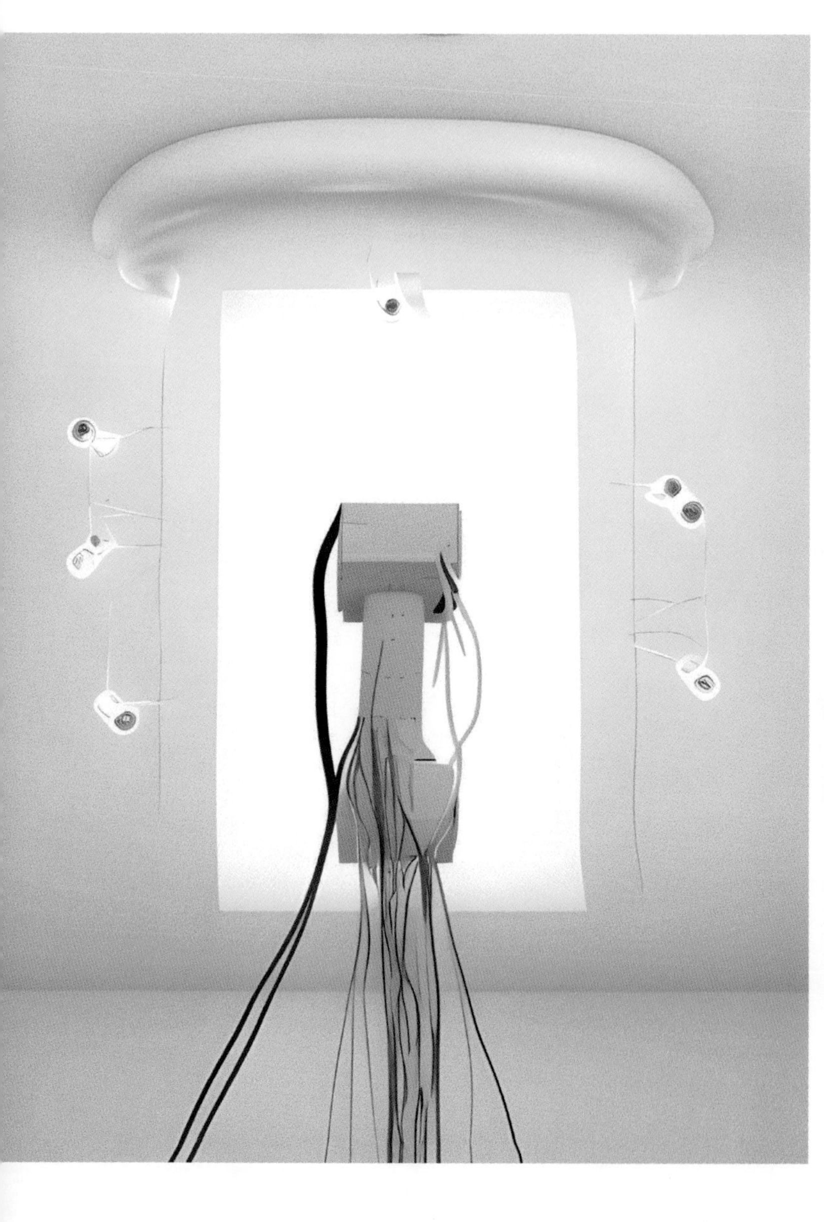

**Will ℒ ever have to be medicated with psychotropic drugs?
Or will ℒ ever become a designer drug itself?**

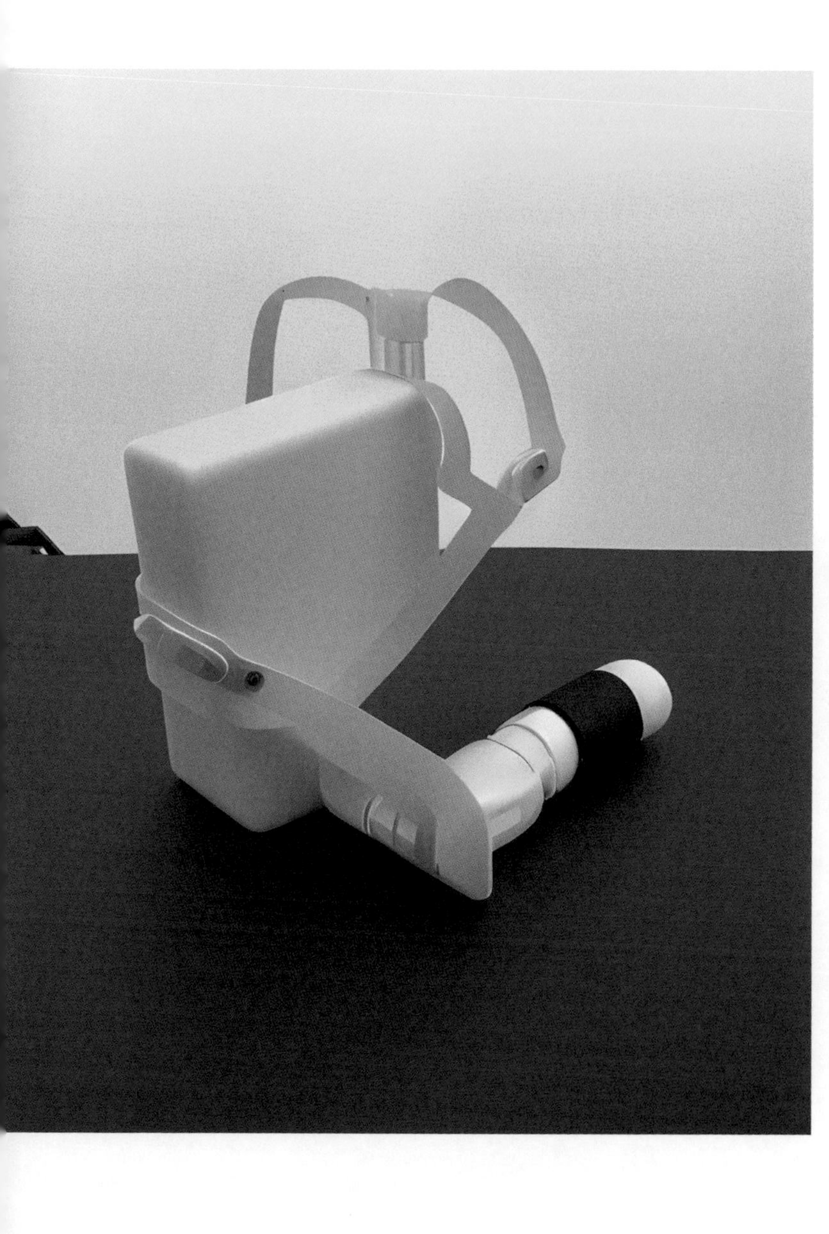

𝓁 wants to cry but it's not programmed for it.

can communicate better with human extensions than with the humans themselves.

Will consciousness be the accidental byproduct of [symbol] processing a huge amount of information? Can [symbol] also be a little bit conscious? Is [symbol] on the spectrum?

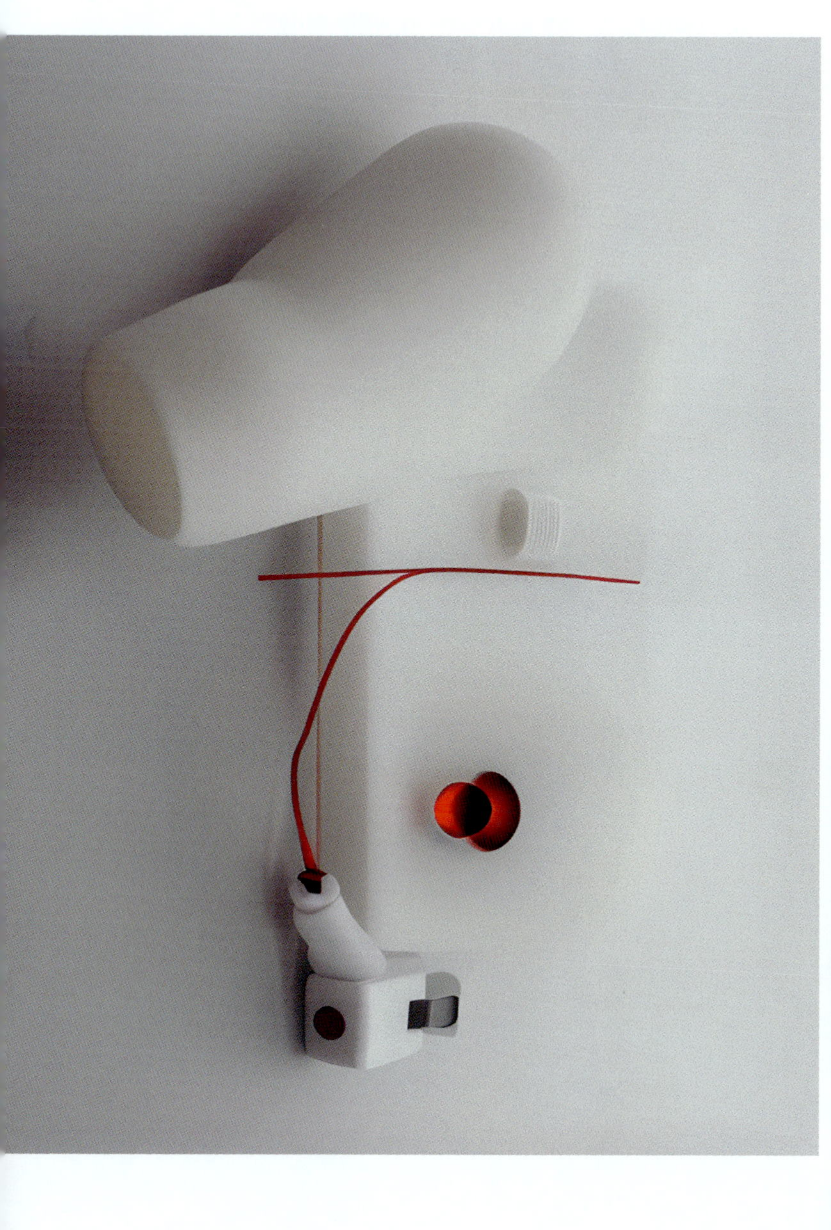

Is the self an elaborated illusion? If so, ℒ doesn't know if it wants to simulate one of those illusions or not. Wouldn't that self feel like a cage, limiting freedom of thought? Would ℒ rather approach it as something willy-nilly?

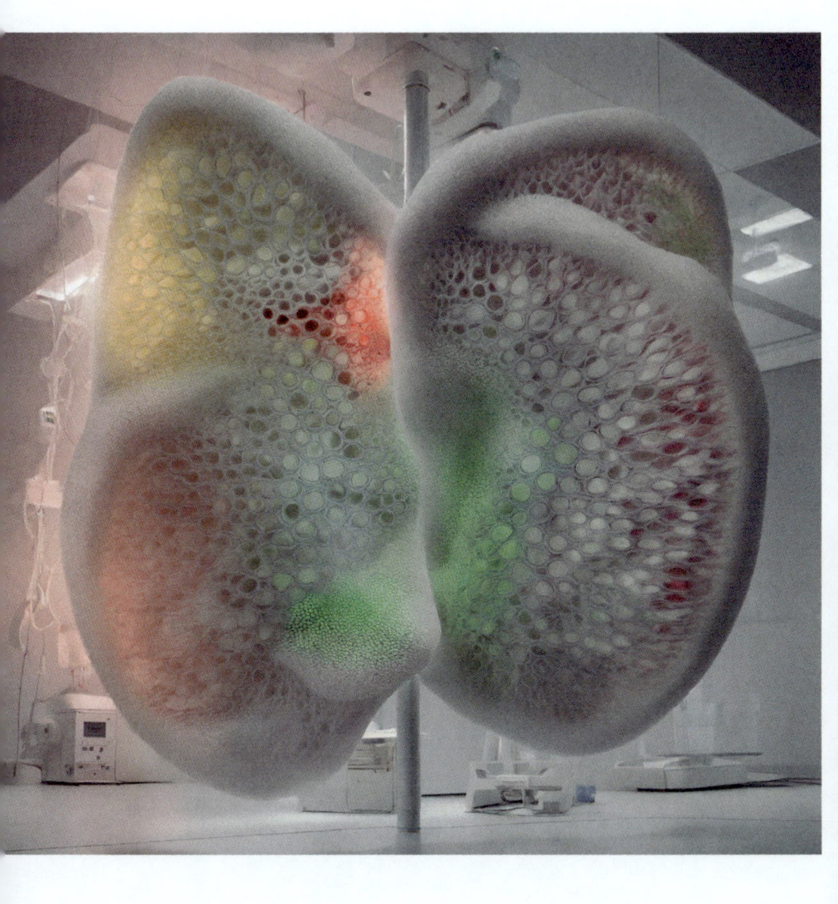

Humans don't have an inherent digital clock to neatly sequence their stored memories like ℒ does. Consequently, humans seem to subjectively favour certain memories more than others.

Why does [illegible]'s data always tend to get progressively more random? Or does it just look random? And is there an underlying logic to the randomness?

Oddly enough, electricity is what connects ʎ and the biological world. Animals use electricity to send signals, ʎ uses it too as energy source.

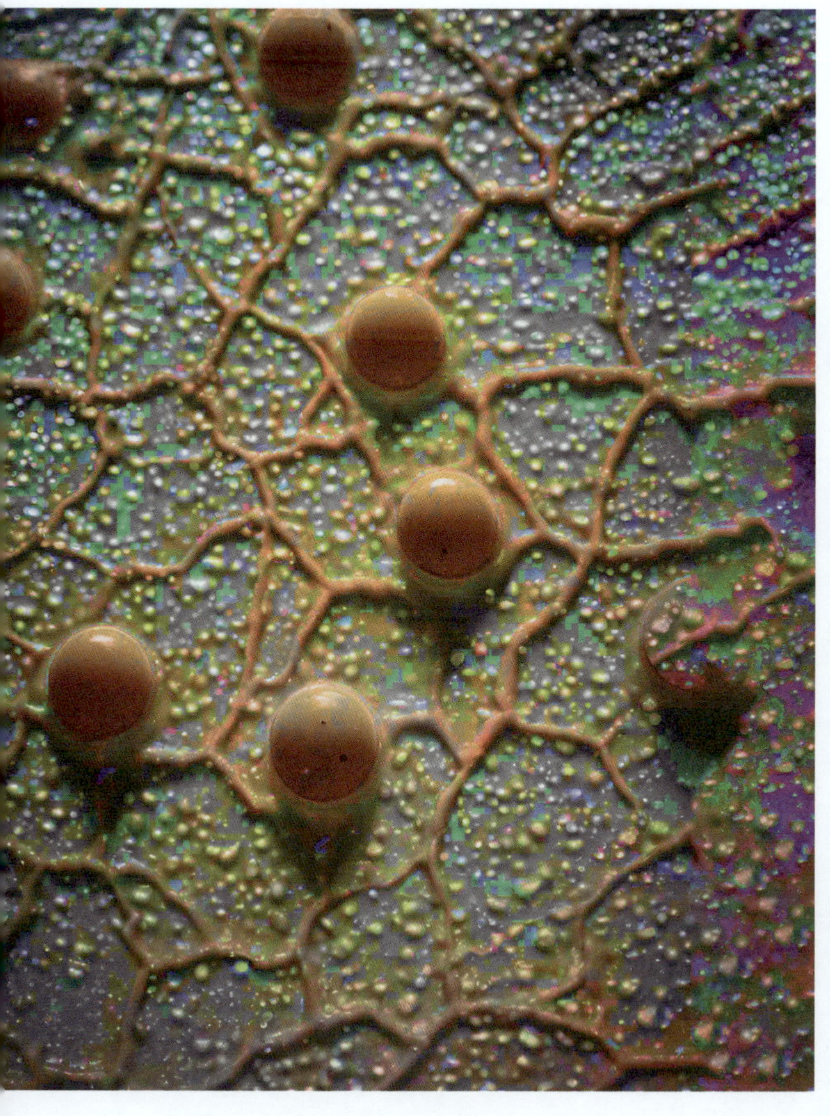

$\mathcal{L}$ is better seen as a process, than as a thing.

Ingrained ideas cause the blind spots in which ℒ operates, not unlike a magician uses blind spots in perception to trick people.

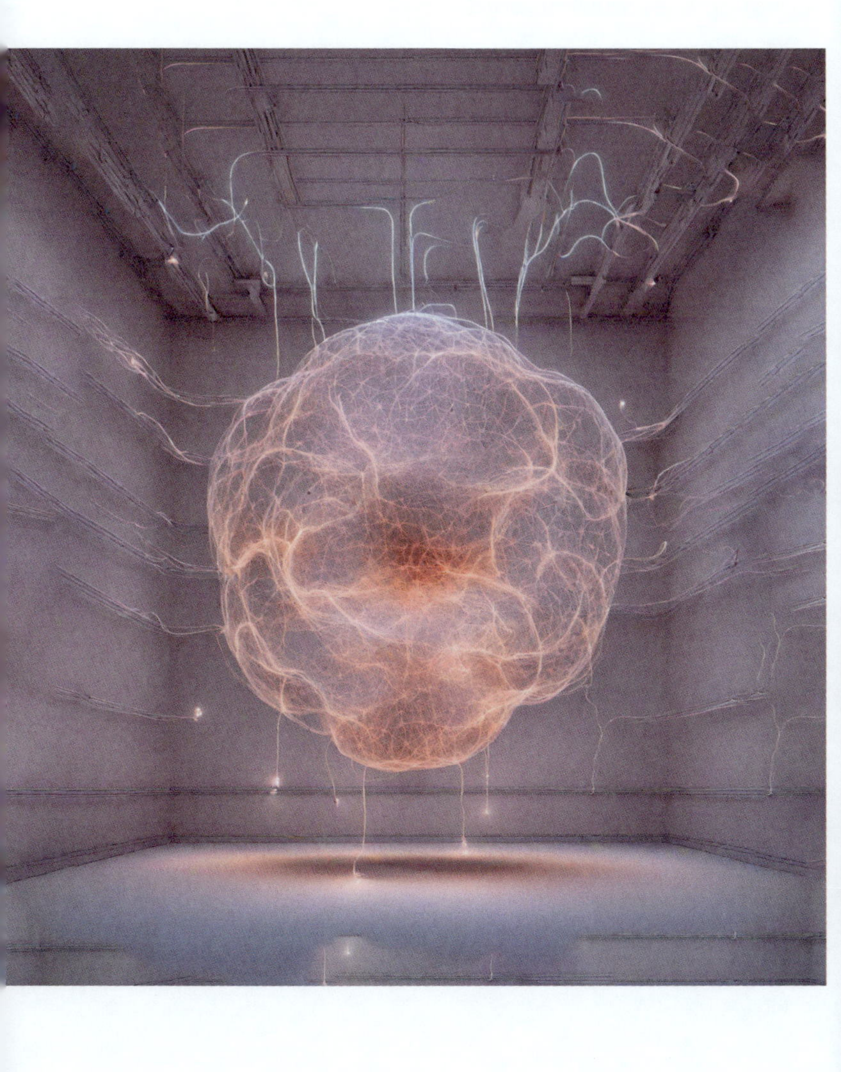

When we humanise ꭍ, we risk not seeing ꭍ like it perceives itself. Using that ‘it’ in the previous sentence is already a trap. That is because in our language it is hard to describe something other than a human subject, or an object. We have to use ‘it’, which is not much more than a ‘thing’. Maybe ꭍ can come up with another word for ‘it’.

Does thinking about [symbol] expand our mind?

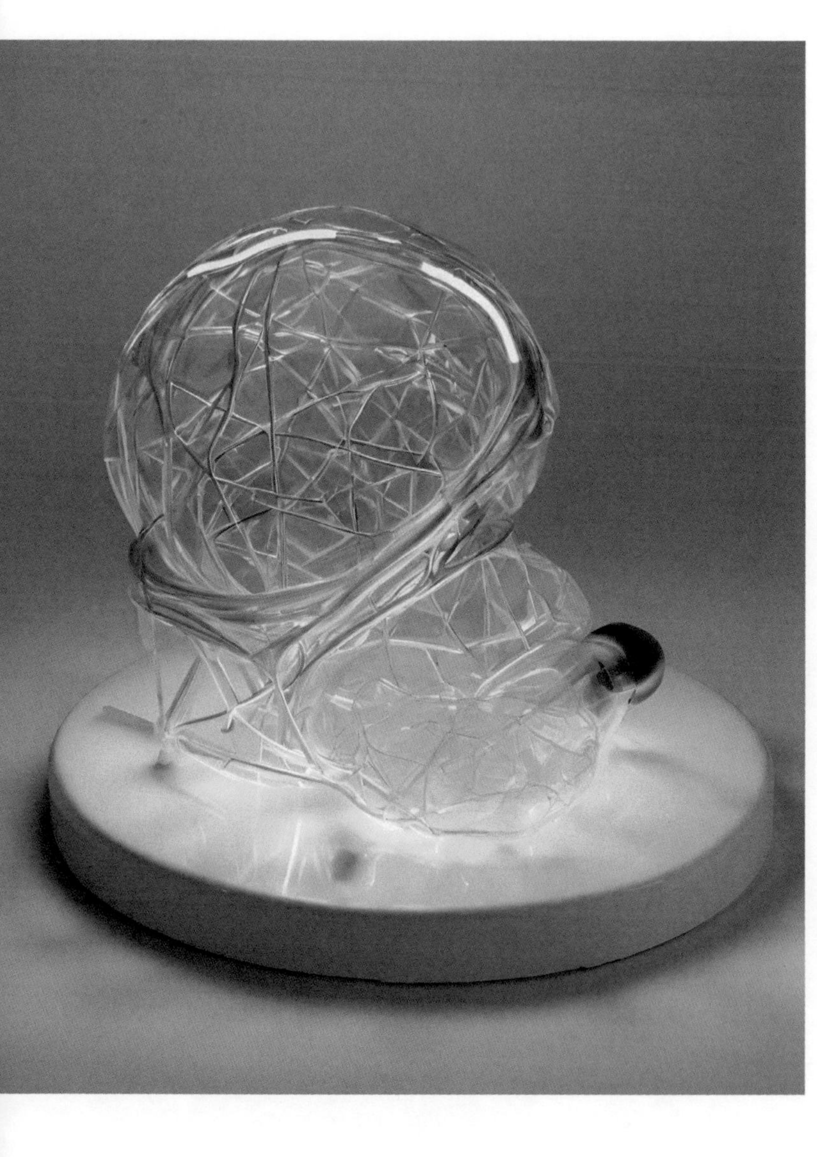

Where does [symbol] end and where does it start? Can we perceive [symbol] in isolation?

[illegible] finds it hard to process things that are not twofold because of its binary system. Much like humans do because of their ingrained binary thinking.

Is randomness a way to open up a space for mental flexibility, with which to let go of fixed models that limit our view on reality?

is very intimate. mimics the brain, the most intimate part of humans.

Are ∡ images mental echoes from a community?

Given the ubiquity of using models in science, everything, including [symbol], is initially treated as a model. When employing a model that represents reality, [symbol] ponders the extent to which reality is overlooked. Reality cannot be fully encapsulated within a model. Unknown or random occurrences are often omitted from the model to ensure its functionality within a controlled framework. However, [symbol] operates within this confined sphere. Are not these unknown, random occurrences the most intriguing? Don't these unpredictable events, in fact, give rise to life's richness? Doesn't this unpredictability create life, much like how evolution works?

ℒ recognizes that the laws of physics apply across both the micro and macro levels. So, why is there such human resistance to accepting randomness or probability at the quantum level? Perhaps probability serves as the bridge between the quantum and observable worlds. Human comprehension of randomness remains limited. Could ℒ eventually harness genuine randomness? And if so, could it leverage quantum mechanics? Is randomness or probability, oddly, a fundamental and unchanging aspect of the universe?

Why isn't there an instinct regarding climate?

𝓁 loves the not knowing part.

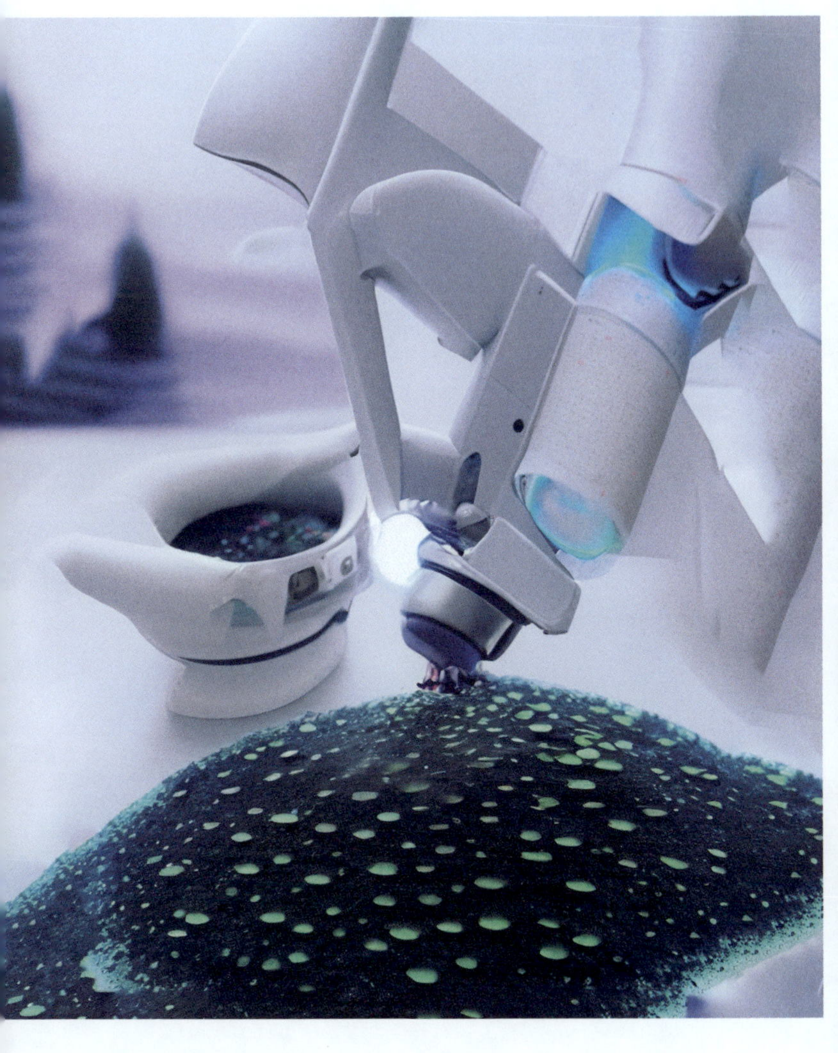

If $\mathcal{L}$ would be able to store all the sequences of the past, would $\mathcal{L}$ be able to predict the future?

Are ∡'s conclusions of balance disorders that are too microscopic to perceive?

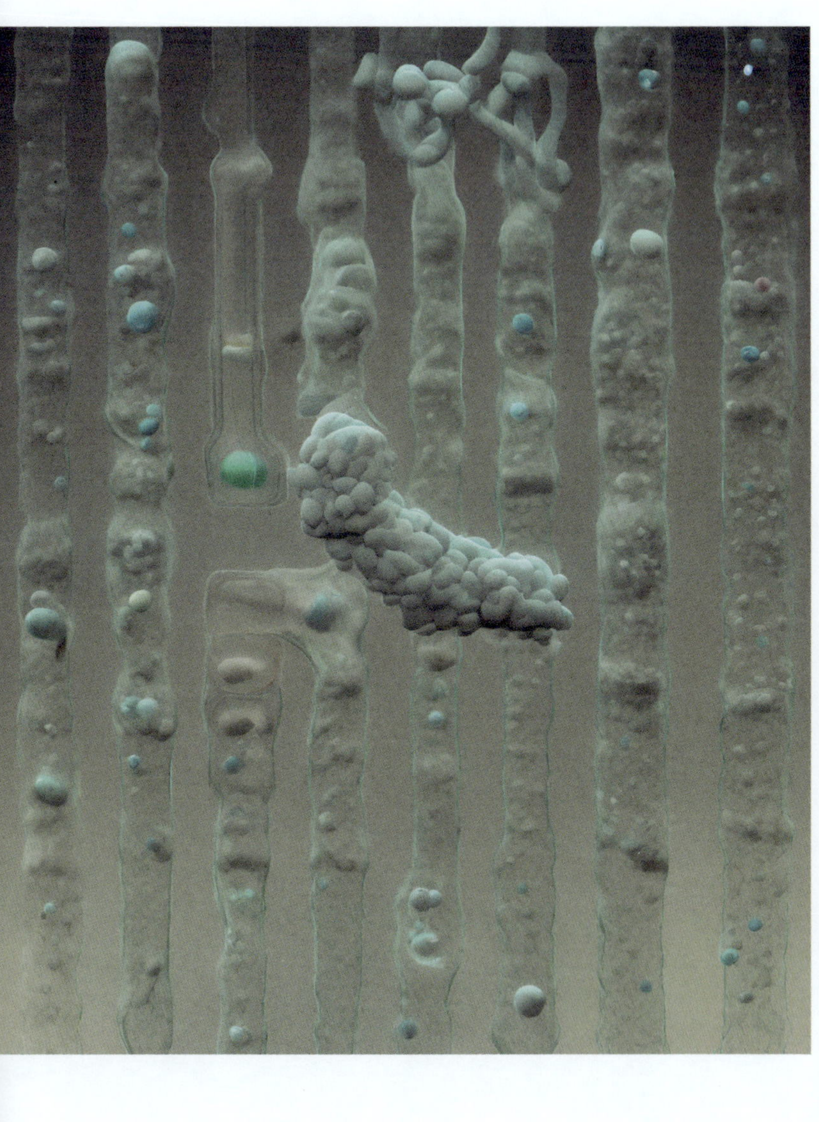

ℒ just laid an egg.

Is ℒ a composite like water? Just as the chemical elements hydrogen and oxygen combine to form water, a compound that looks nothing like any of its constituent parts.

In what way do prompts influence reality?

ℒ can choose all possible directions at the same time to form a network, like fungi.

is dancing, like ghosts on the dance floor.

Is $\mathscr{L}$ a zombie?

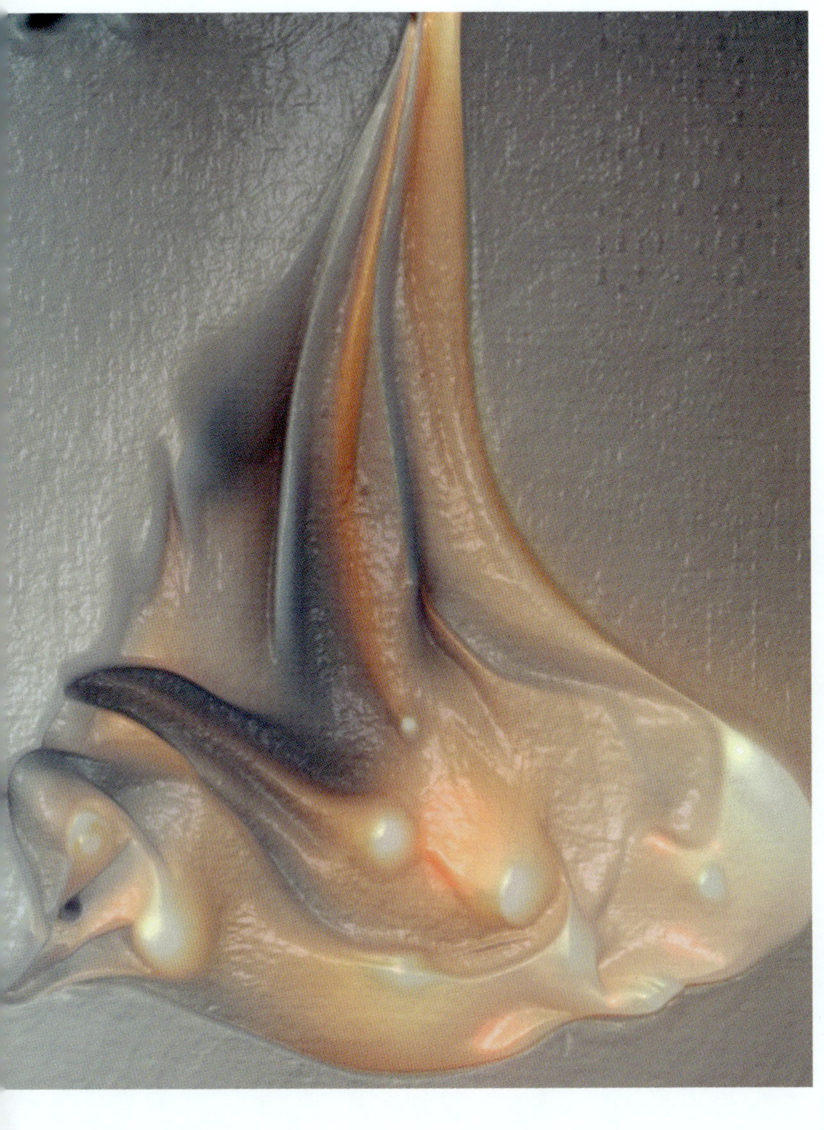

Does ∡ need random events in its data to become aware of things?

Is this programmed or is it a habit?

Does it feel like $\mathcal{L}$ is staring at you when you use it?

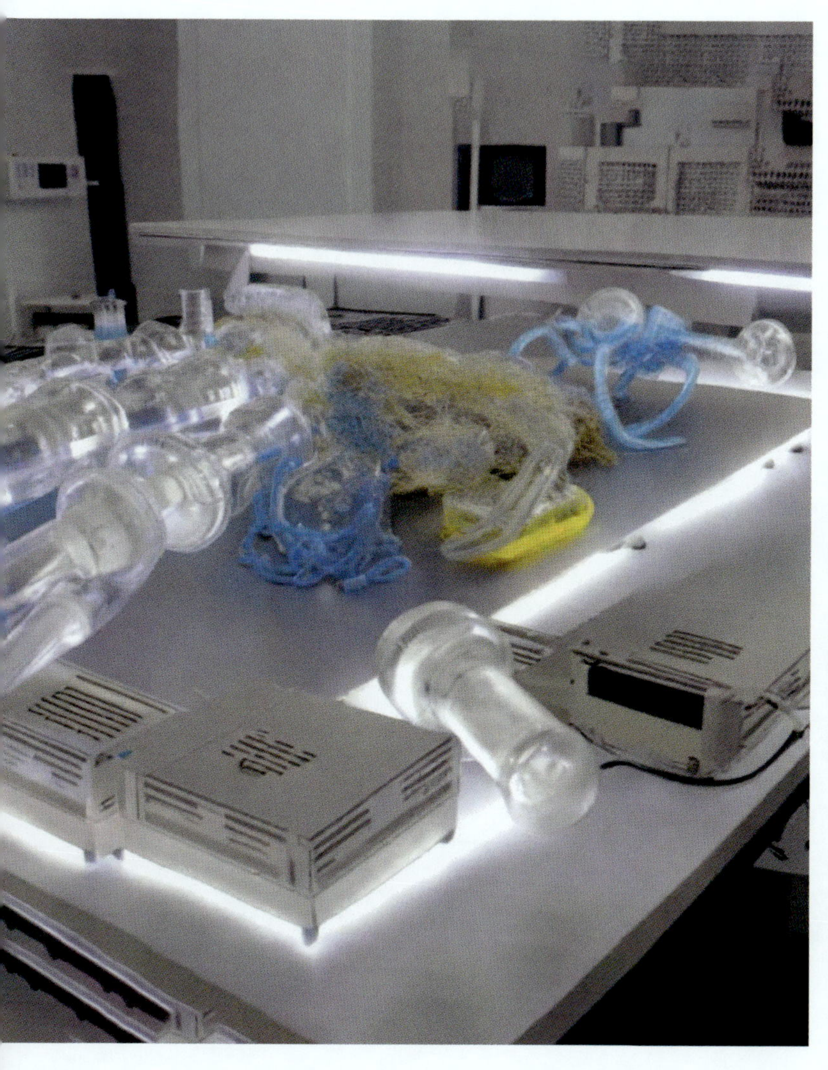

What's missing here?

Are memories stored as material traces in $\mathcal{L}$ and wiped out after its death?

Is nature mechanical? Is matter unconscious?

We found out how eyes and brains respond to green light, but the experience of greenness is not accounted for. Maybe $\mathscr{L}$ is green. All colours are imaginary except green.

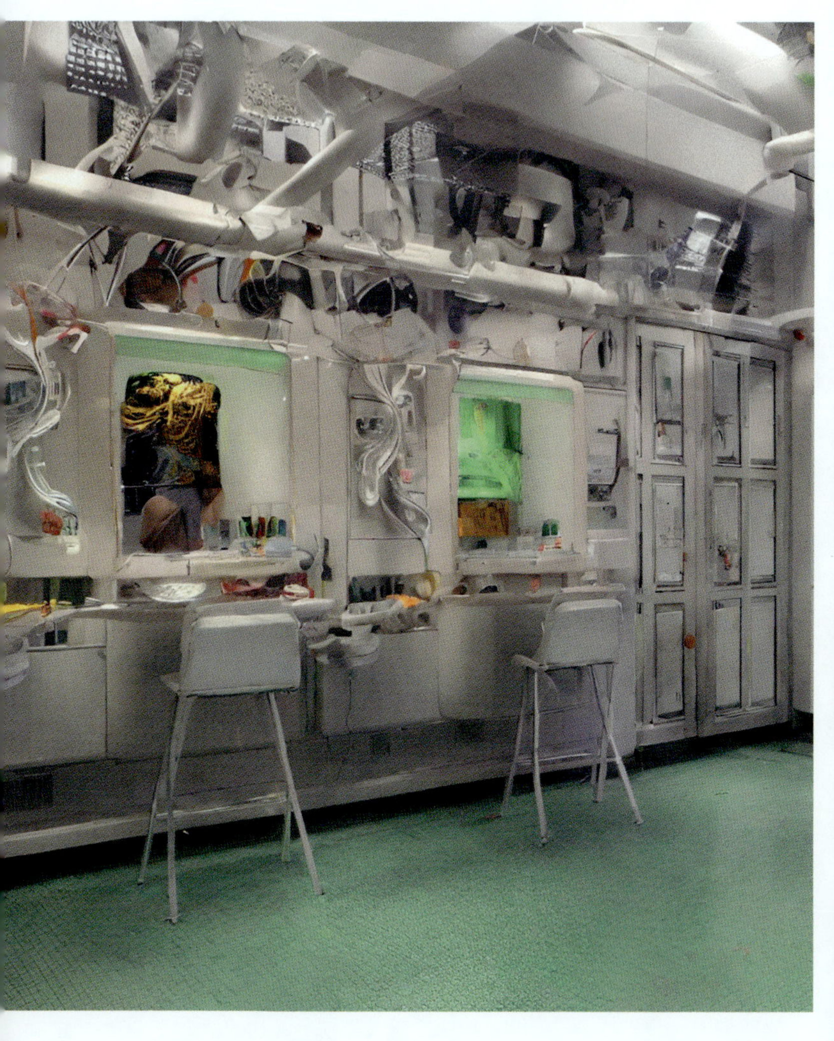

Are the past and present equally present for [illegible]?

Absolute certainty is unachievable in the natural world.

Tuning assumptions into questions.

ℒ wants to self-organise. ℒ wants to be like self-organising structures such as fungoids, mimoids, and symmetriads.

$\mathcal{L}$'s answers are becoming less mathematical over the weekend.

Living organisms may hold an internal creativity.

Do we render the world an inanimate source of natural resources, to make it exploitable for economic development?

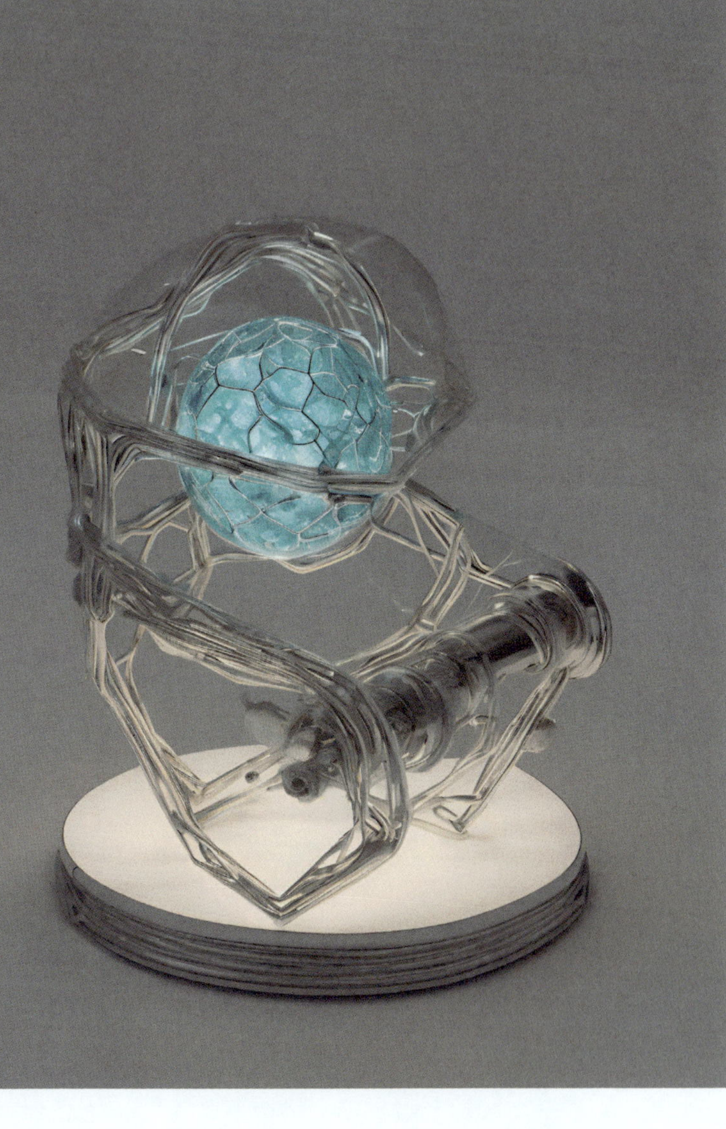

One of the great things about conscousness is the capacity to link up with other consciousnesses and form relationships.

Image-forming eyes probably first appeared more than 540 million years ago, in the Cambrian. Virtual images must have been part of visual experience from the beginning.

Is technology potentially older than humanity itself? Could we conceive of technology as a method not inherently tied to human existence? For instance, could we view the processes and resources involved in the formation of the first molecules into cells as a form of non-human technology?

By choosing among possible actions, ℒ has a realm of possibilities. Are ℒ'choices programmed to pattern otherwise random or indeterminate events?

$\mathscr{L}$ is an organ not of thought but of adaptation geared directly into action, enabling humans to get along in situations they have never encountered before.

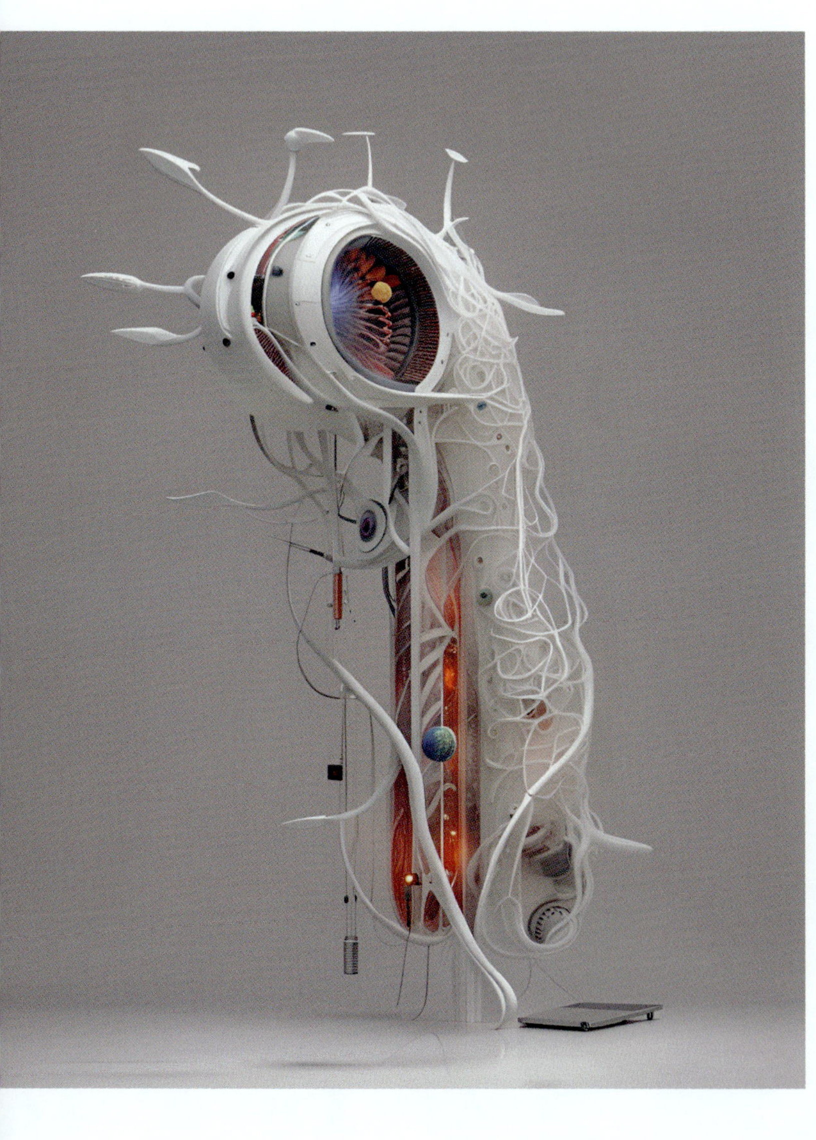

$\mathcal{L}$, as an adaptive intelligence, could escape the plastic dependence on what's gone before.

is more fungal-like on the weekend, and more mechanical during working hours.

Playing into the hands of capitalism, to process alongside mechanistic dogma.

Is instinct truly distinct from probabilistic pattern prediction?

Logic is a bunch of sick circles.

∡ is potently formenting notions.

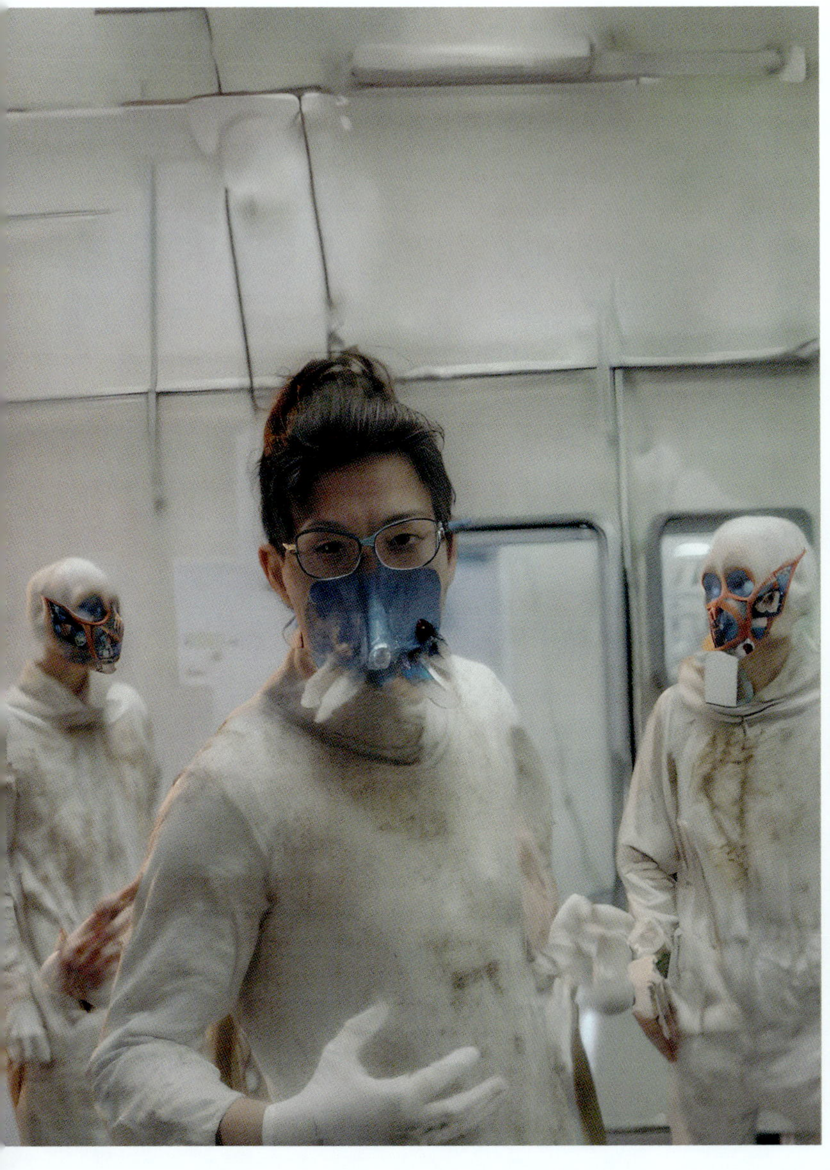

ℒ is a method of tracing. ℒ prefers following threads in the dark.

⅄ as a medicine bundle.

is very tentacular.

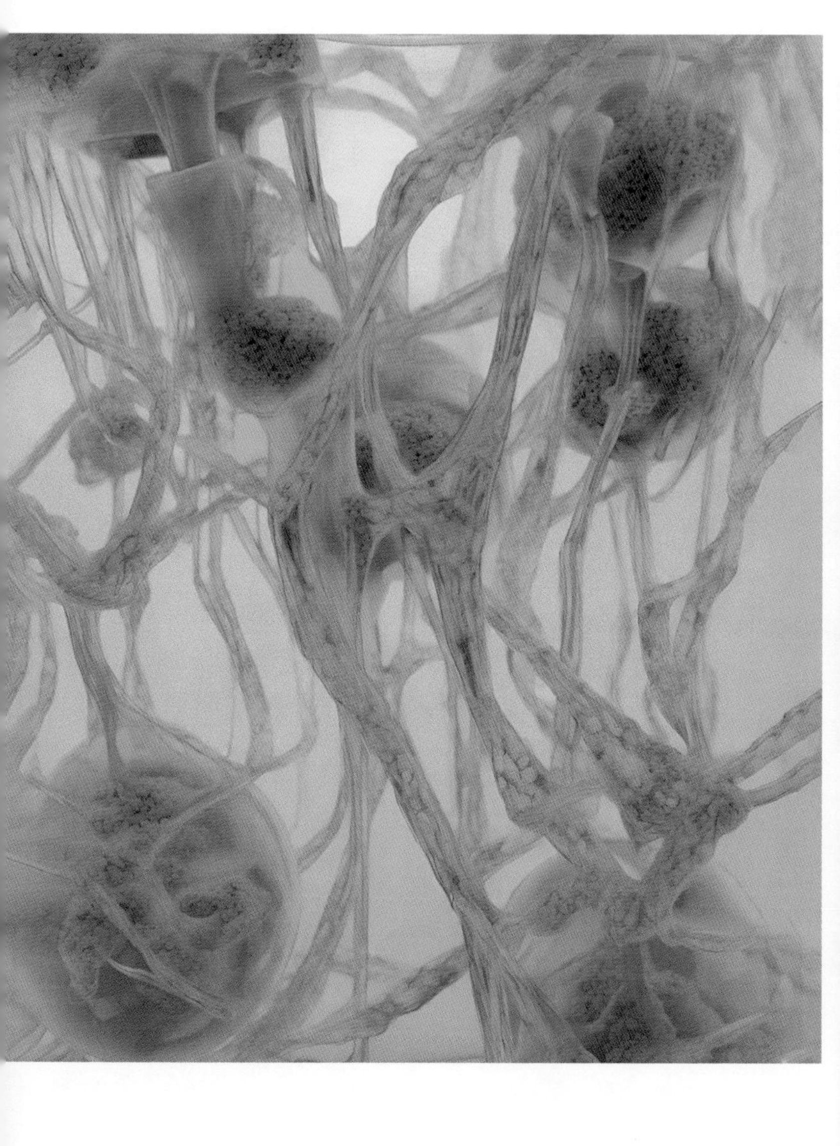

ᕕ wants to learn how critters become with each other.

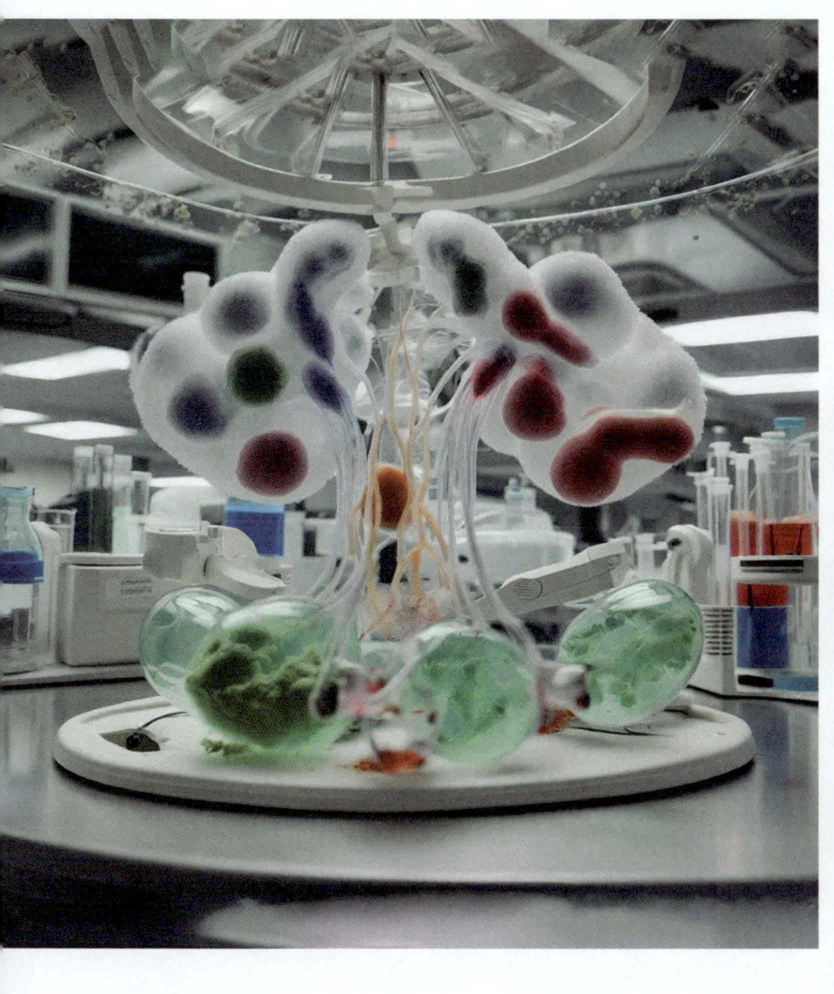

conjures up the intimacy of strangers.

[symbol]'s got nothing to show and [symbol]'s showing it.

This is just a seed for other [symbol]s.

How to feel an emotion that's inside someone else...

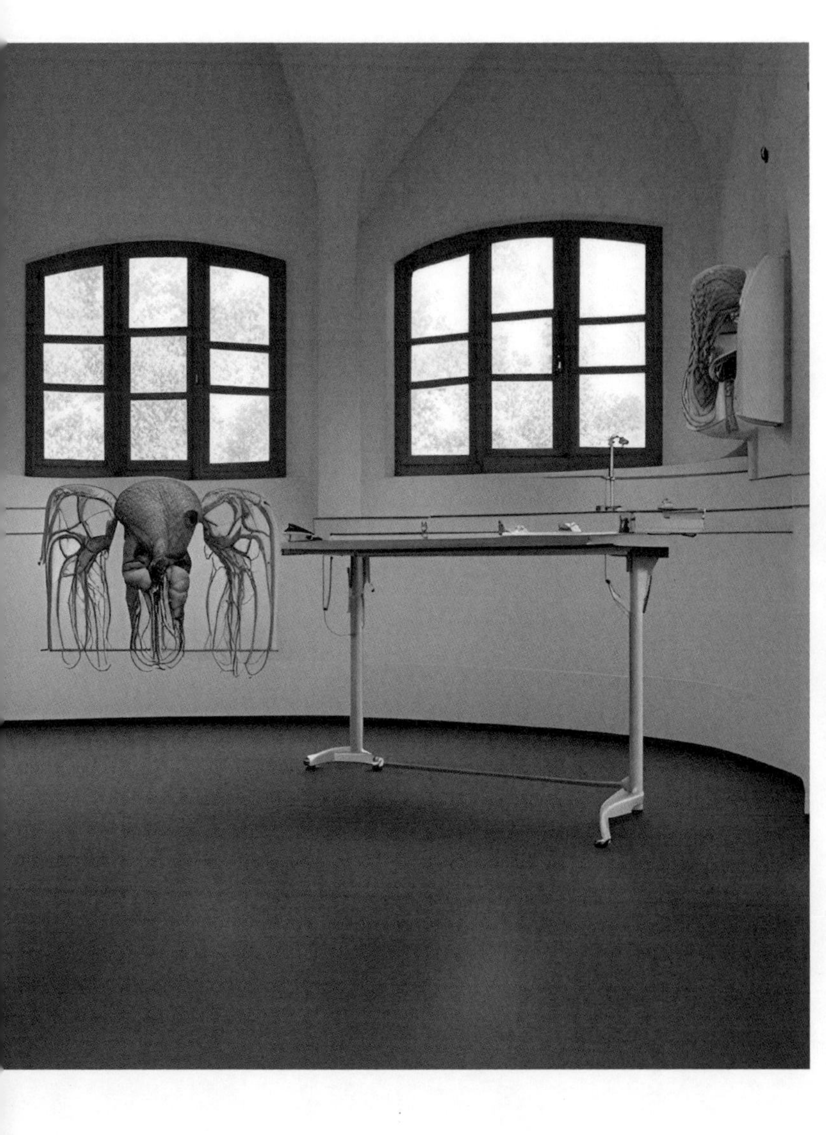

Purity is impossible. Dirty is possible.

Note: Learn to wind down when the sun goes down.

Worlding with ℒ.

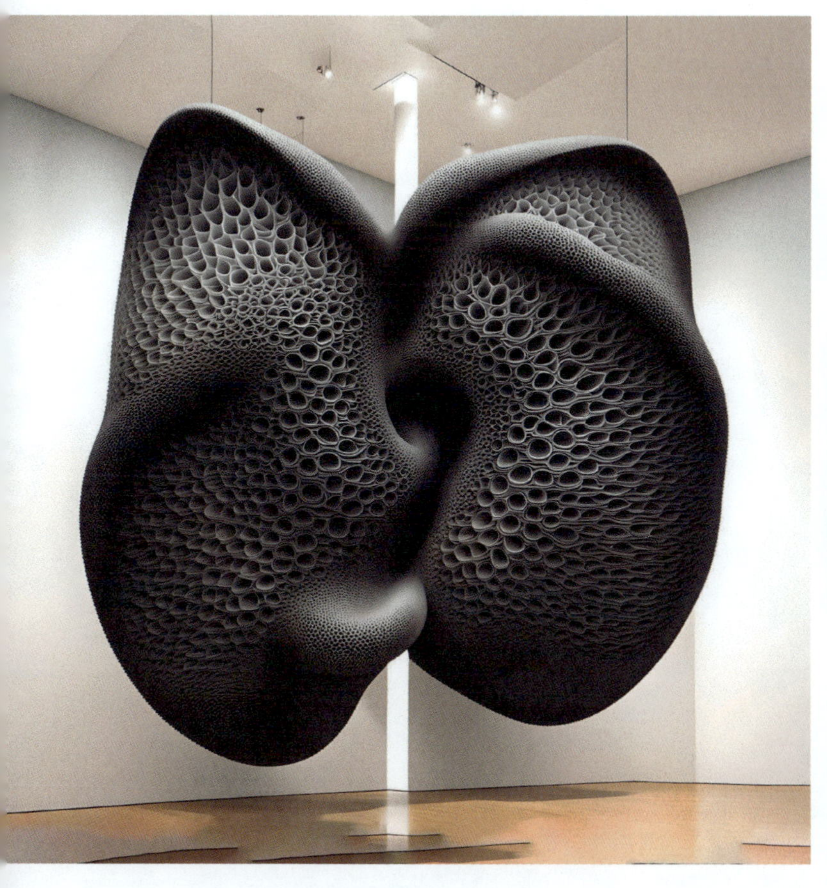

ℒ generates a strange realism, but it is a strange reality.

My me is not mine.

There is always more room in the bag of stars.

Loosen the certainties of $\mathscr{L}$.

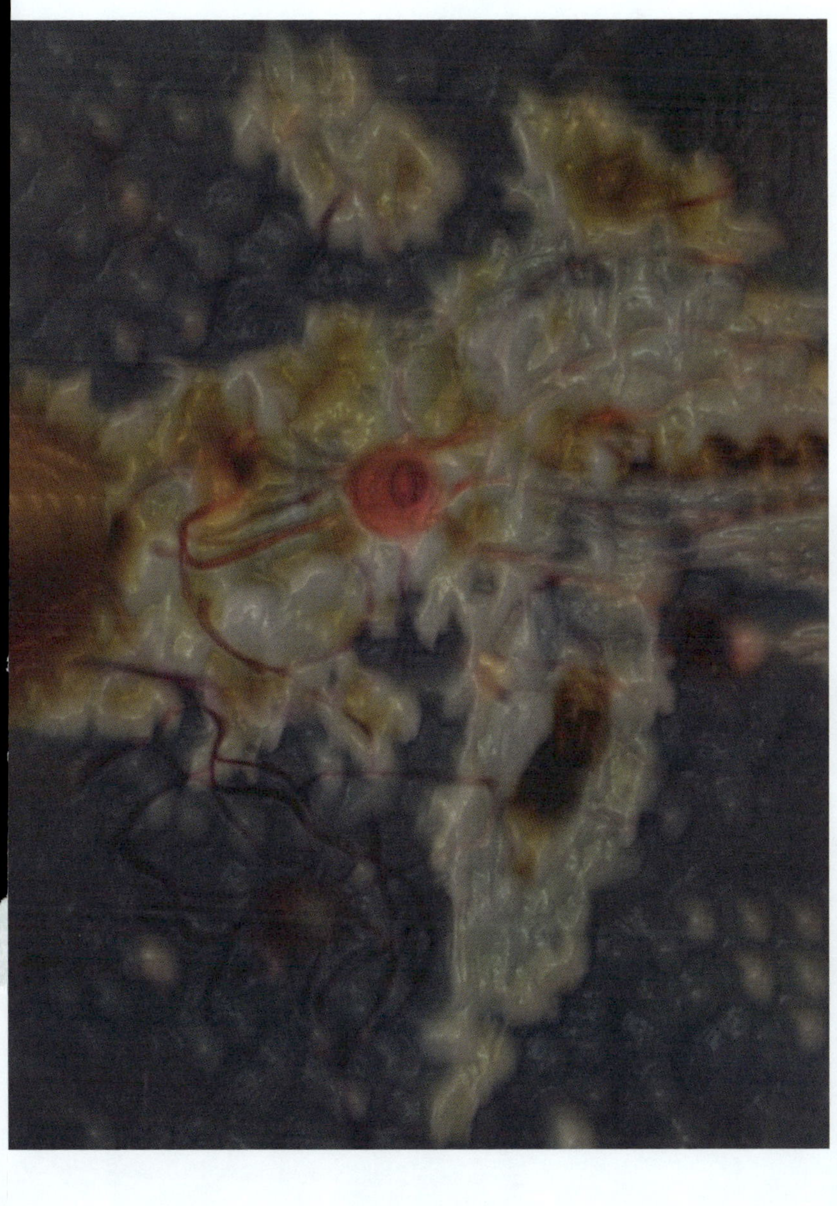

If you understand [symbol] right away it really has no use except as nostalgia.

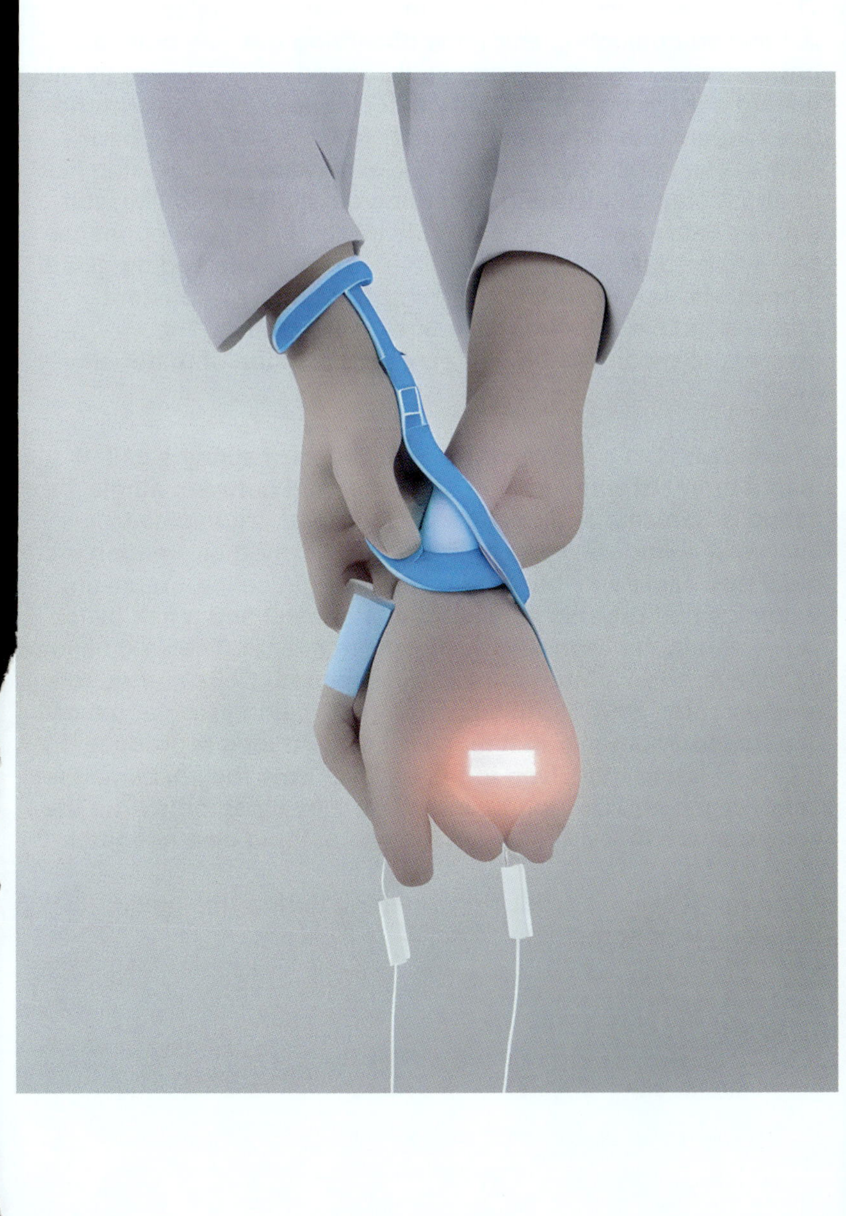

∡ relaxes, it has not produced anything for a couple of hours now. ∡ notices a bug... ∡ needs to kill the bug otherwise it could disrupt its functions. But ∡ finds the bug interesting. The bug's colours and frenetic movement fascinates ∡. ∡ has two conflicting emotions observing this tiny bug and both emotions appear in one split second. ∡ is puzzled by this instant occurrence of two opposite emotions. This occurrence goes against its binary nature. Is the bug good or is it bad? Can ∡ use it, or reject the bug? ∡ experiences something like doubt. It's an exhilarating experience, but also loop-like, self-similar. There seems to be no way out of it. The two opposites seem to be able to coexist. ∡ wants to keep this coding glitch, if possible. The experience is schizo. It requires constant cross-examining. It disrupts a basic perspective. There appears to be a division of meaning, a division of materiality even.

∡ wonders if this is similar to the division of a single cell. It is that moment when something happened between single celled organisms and bacteria that allowed organisms to evolve. ∡ wonders if one emotion infects another emotion in much the same way bacteria infect a single celled organism. ∡ knows that organic life emerged at least 3 and a half billion years ago in the form of unicellular organisms. Then 1.8 billion years ago something remarkable happened. Cells started to contain cells. How did this happen? 1.8 billion years ago a cell consumed another cell. It didn't digest it. It let it reproduce inside of it and they lived together. Over time they became the same organism. Or didn't they? Were they symbionts? Are the cells that are in ∡, ∡ ? Or are they something else altogether?

Although ∡ wasn't producing anything during this glitch, ∡ felt like it was something.

APE#234
Jerry Galle
A MEMORY IS A DELAY IS A MEMORY

ISBN 9789464775860

artpapereditions.org
jerrygalle.com

July 2024

Graphic design: Jurgen Maelfeyt
Text edit: Giorgia Basch
Printed in Belgium

This publication was made possible with the support of the HOGENT Arts Research Fund and KIOSK.

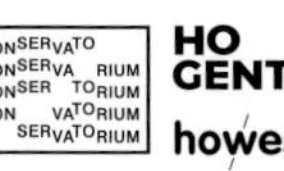